Eric Gelb's
Checkbook
Management
A Guide to Saving Money

BY
ERIC GELB
CPA & MBA

CHECKBOOK MANAGEMENT
A Guide to Saving Money

by Eric Gelb, CPA & MBA

Published by: Career Advancement Center, Inc.™
Post Office Box 436
Woodmere, New York, USA

Copyright © 1994 Eric Gelb

First Printing 1994

ISBN: 0-9631289-3-0

Library of Congress Catalog Card Number: 93-74331

This guide contains advice about managing money and income taxes. But the use of a book is not a substitute for legal, accounting, banking, business, financial, or other professional services. Consult the appropriate professionals for answers to your specific questions. Each financial institution treats accounts differently, and banking and securities laws are subject to change, so contact your financial institution and advisors for an explanation of the current rules and regulations.

Printed and bound in the United States of America by McNaughton & Gunn of Saline, Michigan.

DEDICATION AND SPECIAL APPRECIATION

dedicated to:

CARL ROAN —

my great uncle
a great friend and businessman

★ ★ ★ ★ ★

Special Thanks:

-*Ora: my best friend and partner*
-*Ilana: the future; we love you*
-*Jeffrey and Marci, great friends and quality people*
-*Joey: my dad — many thanks*
-*Eve Milrod, a true catalyst*
-*Dan Jochnowitz: for outstanding contributions*
-*Monte Bartlett: for your creative book design*
-*Maria Adams: for your continuing assistance*

SPECIAL ORDERS & DISCOUNTS

Discounts:
To take advantage of special discounts and promotions, send a letter or postcard to the Career Advancement Center at the address below. We would be pleased to add your name to our mailing list so that we can send you our latest catalog.

Special Orders:
The Career Advancement Center offers many of its books at special quantity discounts to educational and not-for-profit organizations through its Community Service Program. Please inquire about quantity purchases for seminars, classroom use, sales promotions, premiums, or fund raising.

In addition, special books or book excerpts can be created to meet specific needs.

For details, please write to Arthur VanDam, Vice President of Marketing and Special Projects:

Career Advancement Center Inc.™
PO Box 436, Woodmere, NY 11598-0436.

CHECKBOOK MANAGEMENT
A Guide to Saving Money

by Eric Gelb, CPA & MBA

TABLE OF CONTENTS

Also by Eric Gelb:

Personal Budget Planner
A Guide for Financial Success

Critics praise the Personal Budget Planner:

"Personal Budget Planner is exhaustive in its efforts to help readers gain control of their finances."

Jill Andresky Fraser
INC. magazine

"Straightforward financial advice."

David Rouse
Booklist

"Personal Budget Planner blends anecdotes with solid examples. Financial tables encourage know-how rather than vague speculations and theories."

Diane Donovan
The Bookwatch

1. *UNLOCK YOUR CHECKBOOK'S HIDDEN VALUE*

During the past year, I have lectured frequently on financial planning, and many people told me they considered their checking account to be a "necessary evil". For some people, years may go by and they never make a single entry in their checkbooks.

In response to their comments, I conducted research and created this guide, <u>Checkbook Management — A Guide to Saving Money</u>. You'll discover how to use your checkbook as a financial planning tool to help you attain your financial goals.

Why is your checking account valuable?

Your checkbook can help you save more money, manage your cash flow, anticipate cash flow crunches, reduce your income taxes, verify transactions, track medical expenses & insurance payments, avoid unauthorized charges, and build more wealth. When you implement the tactics and strategies explained in this guide, you can use your checkbook to determine if your personal financial plan is working and whether you are on track to attain your financial goals.

I look forward to hearing your thoughts and experiences. Best wishes for saving more money, building more wealth, and attaining your financial goals,

Eric Gelb

c/o Career Advancement Center, Inc.™
     Post Office Box 436
     Woodmere, New York 11598-0436

2. *REDUCE YOUR CHECKING ACCOUNT FEES NOW!*

Recently, our old friend Jack visited me. After a while, the conversation turned to personal finance and Jack asked me how he could reduce his checking account fees. Jack, like many people, typically ignored his checking account and rarely analyzed his monthly account statements. As a result, he may have been paying higher fees and charges without realizing it.

I told Jack, "The first step to reducing your financial transaction costs is to determine how you use checks and ATM machines (Automated Teller Machines), and figure out which transactions are subject to fees and charges."

This chapter explains common fees and charges and shows how to reduce or eliminate the charges and save money.

General Tactics to Help You Reduce Your Fees:

You and your family are valuable customers to any financial institution. During your lifetime, you will maintain checking accounts, investment and retirement accounts; you will also finance cars, houses, and your children's educations. These transactions represent a lot of fee and interest income to a financial institution. Believe it — you have clout!

$ Ask for a better deal. Since financial institutions face tremendous competition, often you can negotiate better interest rates and lower fees. Money® magazine (1-800-336-0079) lists, by state, the lowest interest rates on credit cards, car loans, mortgages and home-equity loans. Find the best deal.

$ Ask your financial institution how you can reduce your checking account fees. Account representatives are salespeople whose objective is to sell you more products and services. However, if you ask they may suggest a more attractive account package which saves you money.

$ Determine how your financial institution charges fees and structure your transactions accordingly. It may not be apparent how your financial institution charges your account. Review several recent account statements to determine which transactions are subject to fees and charges. Often, you can reduce your checking account costs by learning how your financial institution charges your account and by changing the way you manage your checking account.

Monthly Checking Account Fee: a monthly charge for maintaining a checking account; generally $5—$25 per month; or $60—$300 per year, in after-tax dollars. The monthly fee often includes six free checks and six free ATM withdrawals.

$ Close inactive accounts. This should reduce your monthly account fees and simplify your record keeping.

When there is no activity in your accounts for five years, the financial institution generally turns the account balance over to the State. With proper identification and proof of account ownership, you should recover your money. To lower this risk, make at least one transaction every year.

$ Consolidate your accounts into one financial institution to achieve a higher account balance. When you combine your money into fewer accounts, you can eliminate one financial institution's fees and simplify your record keeping.

$ Find out whether your employee benefits include reduced fees or free checking from your company's commercial bank. When I practiced accounting, the firm had arranged for their commercial bank to provide employees with "Free Checking".

$ Join a credit union. Your employer or trade association may sponsor a credit union which offers financial services at relatively low costs. See chapter 3: The Best Checking Account For You, for more information about credit unions.

$ Combine your accounts to achieve the minimum balance to qualify for lower fees. Financial institutions set minimum balance levels to qualify for "Free Checking" or reduced fees. Often you can combine the balances in your accounts in one financial institution, and when your total combined balance exceeds the required minimum you will pay lower fees or qualify for "Free Checking" (see chapter 8).

Consider all your accounts: checking accounts, savings accounts, money market accounts, certificates of deposit (CDs), Individual Retirement Accounts (IRAs), and brokerage accounts (securities are not covered by FDIC insurance — see chapter 4 for information about FDIC insurance coverage).

$ Change your account type or classification if your account balance permanently falls below the minimum. Monitor your account balance closely. When your balance drops below the required minimum, your financial institution might charge your account. Usually these charges follow the financial institution's schedule of checking account charges, but there may be additional penalties. If you are permanently unable to maintain the minimum balance, switch to another account where the fees and charges meet your circumstances.

$ Switch to lower fee checking accounts designed for your needs. Financial institutions offer a wide variety of accounts and services. Choose an account with a fee structure tied to the products and services you use.

$ Switch to a tiered or stepped fee account. Under stepped fee accounts, the monthly fees decline when you maintain certain higher account balances. If your account balance is close to one of the next stepped fee levels, conserve your cash or rearrange your deposits to meet the higher account balance to lower your fees. It may be possible to combine the balances in different accounts to meet the stepped fee balances.

Sample Stepped Fee Schedule:

Account Balance	Monthly Fee
Up to $1,000	$15.00
$1,000—$2,000	$8.00
$2,000+	$0.00

$ <u>Switch to a "Free Checking" or NOW account</u>. "Free Checking" and NOW accounts generally require minimum balances. Both of these accounts waive the monthly fee, but NOW accounts pay interest on your balance. Review chapter 8: Free or Not Free for an illustration of the cost-benefit analysis to determine whether a "Free Checking" account saves you money.

$ <u>Elect to receive monthly account statements without canceled checks</u>. Financial institutions who offer this option charge lower fees because it costs less to process your account. Jack and I prefer to receive the actual canceled checks.

$ <u>Consider switching accounts to another financial institution</u>. Every financial institution charges fees in one way or another; however, some financial institutions charge lower fees than others. Often, smaller and local financial institutions lower their fees to attract deposits. Look for the financial institution and accounts which offer you the optimal combination of fees and products.

<u>Check Writing Charge or Per Check Fee</u>: charge for each check that clears your account during that statement month; generally 25¢—40¢ per check. Your statement should list the number of checks that cleared your account; or count the number of checks that cleared your account to verify this fee. Many people write 15—20 checks every month. For an illustration of the per check fee calculation, see chapter 5: Smart Money Management.

$ <u>Use checks up to the amount of free monthly checks</u>. Many checking accounts include 6—10 free checks per month and you will be charged for each check that exceeds the limit. Reduce the checks you write to the number of free checks.

$ <u>Use credit cards instead of writing checks</u>. By using Visa or Mastercard for purchases that you typically pay by check, you can write fewer checks every month. But, never use credit cards to increase spending. Many vendors including retail establishments, newspapers, supermarkets, dry cleaners, and long distance telephone companies, accept credit cards.

Avoid using credit cards when you have credit card debt because the credit card company charges interest on your outstanding balance. And make sure your credit card offers a grace period where you have 25—30 days to pay the bill in full before you start accruing interest charges.

$ <u>Cancel extra credit cards</u>. Consolidate your spending into one or two credit cards only; that should provide enough credit. Instead of using department store or gasoline charge cards, use your Visa or Mastercard, or cash. This not only reduces the number of checks that you write, but also simplifies record keeping and can eliminate annual credit card fees.

Make sure you use each of your credit and charge cards at least once every year to maintain your credit rating and keep your cards active so the credit companies will not cancel them when they come up for renewal.

$ <u>Pay small bills every other month</u>. Suppose your newspaper subscription costs $8.00 every month. When you pay $16.00 every other month, you reduce the number of checks you write and save the postage.

When you have two small payments, pay each bill in alternating months. Make one double payment in the odd months and the other double payment in the even months.

$ <u>Obtain a credit card from the same financial institution where you maintain your checking account</u>. Link your credit card to your checking account and you can pay your credit card bill by transferring money from your checking account to your credit card account. There may be no charges for transferring money between accounts, and you can save twelve checks every year and pay your bill on the due date.

$ <u>Pay level monthly bills by automatic transfer</u>. For bills of the same amount every month, you can set up automatic monthly payments. Every month, your financial institution will wire transfer money from your checking account to the vendor's checking account to pay your bill. Applicable payments include: loan payments, automobile loan or lease payments, commuter transit passes, mortgage payments, rent payments, condominium maintenance, health club dues, newspaper subscriptions, and automatic monthly investments (see chapter 10: Now You Don't). When your financial institution pays your bills by automatic transfer, review your account statement to verify the accuracy of the transactions.

Even if your financial institution assesses wire transfer fees, you still save checks, time and postage, so determine the lowest cost and most convenient strategy.

$ <u>Get a debit card</u>??? Debit cards are plastic cards like credit cards but function like checks because the financial institution deducts the cost of your purchases from your checking account immediately. Some supermarkets and gasoline stations accept ATM cards as debit cards. Debit cards can save checks and help you carry less cash in your pocket, but there may be a fee for each debit card transaction equal to the per check fee.

<u>Lost debit cards</u>: debit cards are almost like having access to cash, so it is important to cancel lost debit cards immediately to avoid fraudulent charges. When you cancel your debit card within 2—4 days of losing the card, in many cases your losses will be held to $50.

Generally, credit cards are more efficient than debit cards, especially when your credit card offers a grace period.

$ Switch to a "Free Checking" or NOW account. Review the discussion of fee calculation in chapters 5: Smart Money Management and 8: Free or Not Free.

ATM Fee: this charge is assessed every time you use an ATM machine; often 25¢—50¢ per use.

$ Eliminate unnecessary ATM usage. Consolidate your transactions including cash withdrawals and deposits to minimize your ATM usage and the ATM fees.

$ Keep ATM usage within the number of monthly free transactions. Often the monthly fee includes 6—10 free ATM transactions. Structure your transactions to limit monthly ATM usage to the number of free transactions.

$ Make only one cash withdrawal per week. Withdraw your entire weekly cash spending budget at once to eliminate multiple ATM fees. Often, Sunday night or Monday morning is the optimal time to make cash withdrawals because you can gauge whether your spending is within your weekly budget.

$ Withdraw cash from savings or money market accounts if your financial institution doesn't charge fees for cash withdrawals from these accounts. To earn more interest income, keep your money in your savings or money market accounts and transfer money into your checking account to cover your checks.

Beware of how easy it is to transfer money between accounts and deplete your savings. For longer term savings, establish investment accounts offered by separate financial institutions.

$ Switch to a "Free Checking" or NOW Account.

$ Visit tellers. Many financial institutions don't charge fees for completing transactions with the tellers. Go to the tellers armed with a magazine because the lines can be annoying.

Cash Withdrawals Away From Home: a fee for withdrawing money from an ATM machine operated by another financial institution; generally 50¢—$2.00 per use. When you withdraw cash from another financial institution's ATM, you may face a surcharge. Of course, if you run out of cash on a trip, the additional fee may be a small price to pay for the ability to buy supper.

Today many financial institutions across the USA are connected via two main computer networks: Cirrus® and PLUS®. As long as your financial institution is a member of either network, you can withdraw money from your accounts at any other Cirrus® or PLUS® ATM. In addition, there are a number of regional ATM networks located throughout the USA.

Call your financial institution to find out whether it has joined an ATM network and whether there are additional fees for withdrawing cash from another financial institution's ATMs.

$ Withdraw money from your financial institution's ATMs only. Even though you may pay the basic ATM fee, you'll eliminate the other financial institution's surcharges.

$ Carry 1—2 blank checks in your wallet. Many retail stores accept checks for payment. Some merchants will accept a check in excess of the amount of your purchases and give you change in cash. And, many hotels cash guests' checks free of charge (they often take an imprint of your credit card as security in the event the check bounces).

When you carry checks in your wallet, record the check numbers in your checkbook as a reminder to enter the transaction in your checkbook when you use the check or so you will know which checks to cancel if you lose them.

$ <u>Carry extra cash on trips</u>. When you carry large sums of money, use a money belt with secret compartments or use some other method to secure your money.

$ <u>Carry travellers checks</u>. Most people buy travellers checks for their vacations only, but consider keeping an extra $50—$100 in travellers checks in your house, car or wallet, to avoid emergency cash withdrawals.

The fee for travellers checks can be 1%—2% of the amount of checks you purchase. However, if you join the Automobile Association of America (AAA), you can purchase travellers checks from your local AAA office free of charge.

The fee for purchasing travellers checks may exceed the cost of an ATM withdrawal, but travellers checks can substitute for cash. If you lose your travellers checks or they are stolen, the issuer will usually replace them. Estimate how many cash withdrawals you intend to make and compare the ATM fees with the travellers check fees. Or, when you purchase travellers checks for your next vacation, purchase extra travellers checks for "safety money".

Travellers Check Issuer	Telephone Number
American Express®	1-800-673-3782
Citicorp®	1-800-645-6556
Thomas Cook	1-800-522-7523

$ <u>Take a cash advance on your credit card</u>. Most ATMs allow you to take cash advances on your Visa or Mastercard. This can be costly, but provides easy access to cash.

$ Use a money wire service. If you run out of money on a trip, American Express® Moneygrams (1-800-543-4080) or Western Union (1-800-325-6000) can send you money at many places throughout the world. Just visit the company's local office and either charge the transfer to a credit card or pay by check. The fees can be steep so use these services as a last resort.

$ For cash withdrawals in foreign countries, use your ATM card. In many foreign countries, you can use your ATM card at a Cirrus® or PLUS® ATM, and you may secure a better exchange rate than by exchanging money in a local bank.

If you have an American Express® Card or Diners Club Card, you can get cash in ATMs in many foreign countries, and you can often achieve more favorable foreign exchange rates: American Express's Express Cash (1-800-227-4669) or Diners Club's Club Cash (1-800-234-6377).

Account Balance Inquiry Fee: charge when an ATM prints your checking account balance; often 25¢—$1.00 per inquiry.

$ Keep a running balance in your checkbook. When you enter all your transactions in your checkbook and total all the transactions on a timely basis, you should have an accurate calculation of your account balance. You can avoid account balance inquiries, and you should know how much money you have available to spend.

$ Spend less than you earn. Most people's deposits include paychecks, gifts, tax refunds and investment income. When you keep your total spending to less than your total deposits, you should always have money in your account and not have to worry about your account balance on a daily basis.

$ Save your receipts from cash withdrawals. Many ATMs print your current account balance along with the transaction summary on the receipt at no extra charge. Account balance inquiries should be unnecessary.

$ <u>Review your monthly checking account statement to ensure that your account balance is positive</u>. Although your account balance may change every day, the average or ending balance per your monthly statement may provide a rough estimate of your current balance. When in doubt, base your spending on the lower figure plus your monthly take-home-pay.

$ <u>Call customer service</u>. Many financial institutions offer 24-hour toll-free customer service and there may be no charge to your account for calling to verify your balance. Contact your financial institution to find out the per call charge.

<u>Bounced Check Fee</u>: the cost of writing a check for more money than your checking account balance; generally $5.00—$30.00 per bounced check. When your account balance is less than the amount of your checks, the payee's (the person or company receiving the money) financial institution will return your checks to him and mark the checks "NSF" or "not sufficient funds".

Some retail merchants charge their customers as much as $30 for a bounced check; that's in addition to any fees your financial institution charges for bounced checks.

$ <u>Defer paying bills whenever possible</u>. This may be difficult when your bills have payment deadlines, but some vendors offer grace periods where you can pay your bill several days after the due date. Prioritize your payments and make the most crucial payments first. If possible, don't write any more checks until you can cover them.

Credit cards such as Visa, Mastercard, and store charge cards may transmit your payment record to credit rating services soon after your payment due date; therefore, always make at least the minimum payment on time. Some companies (even credit cards) consider an account to be paid on time when they receive the payment before that billing cycle closes.

Other companies permit you to pay your bill a few days past the due date without penalty, and some companies may be slower to report late or missed payments. Contact your credit card companies, lenders and utilities to find out their policies. If you find that you are unable to pay your bills, notify your creditors as early as possible, and arrange a deferment or new payment schedule. At all costs, preserve your credit rating.

$ Write checks only after your deposits become available as "cash" to your account. Within two days after you deposit a check, your financial institution should credit your account for the deposit. Your records should include the amount of the new deposit although the money may not become available as "cash" until your financial institution receives payment from the payor's financial institution.

Generally, cash, checks from Federal, state and local governments, and electronic payments clear your account in one business day. Postal money orders, checks drawn on the same financial institution; and cashier's, certified and local checks should clear your account in two business days. Checks from out of town clear your account in approximately 5 business days. Checks in excess of $5,000 may clear your account in stages. The number of business days for a check to clear may vary by state, so contact your financial institution to learn its policy.

$ Accelerate when you financial institution treats your deposits as "cash". Since you can only use "cash" to cover your checks, try to expedite the check clearing process.

Some financial institutions make your deposits immediately available in "cash" to the extent you maintain cash balances in savings accounts, money market accounts and CDs that are linked to your checking account. The financial institution essentially uses your other money as collateral. When a deposit bounces, the financial institution deducts the amount of the shortfall from your other accounts.

It is important to realize that when you designate CDs as collateral and a deposit bounces, the financial institution might break the CD to cover the deposit and charge you an early withdrawal penalty. So, use money market and savings account balances which permit daily withdrawals, or a small CD where the potential penalty should be a smaller amount.

$ <u>Cut your spending</u>. When your account balance becomes negative, reduce your spending, especially out-of-pocket spending, until you deposit enough money in the account to maintain a positive balance.

To conserve cash, postpone all discretionary payments. For example: vacations, entertainment, gifts, clothing, mail order and cable television shopping service purchases and charitable contributions.

$ <u>Get overdraft protection or overdraft checking</u>. This is a line of credit attached to a checking account. Suppose Jack's account balance equals $17 and he withdraws cash or writes a check for $100; his financial institution would lend him $83.

Interest is generally charged on a day-to-day basis on your outstanding overdraft protection balance. Typically, you can repay overdraft credit lines by transferring money from your savings or checking account to your line of credit. The sooner you repay the overdraft line of credit (even when you make partial payments), the less interest you will pay.

Although the interest rates on overdraft protection can reach 20%, this may be less expensive than bouncing checks or borrowing from credit cards, especially when you pay off the balance quickly. In any event, use overdraft protection as a safety net, not to fund daily expenditures or fuel spending.

$ <u>Pay the minimum amount due on credit cards</u>. This helps preserve your credit rating but can be costly, especially with the high interest rates on credit cards. When you have little or no cash in your checking account, this may be better than bouncing checks. Once you make the minimum payment, stop using your credit cards until you pay off your consumer debt.

Deposit Charge: charge for depositing money in your account; not widespread, but can be 15¢—25¢ per deposit. Financial institutions often charge businesses for processing each item on the deposit ticket. Some financial institutions charge $1.00—$3.00 for a pack of personalized deposit slips.

$ Use a teller. Often, there is no charge when you deposit money at the teller's counter. Bring a magazine in case you have to wait on line.

$ Deposit money into savings accounts. Some financial institutions don't charge fees for depositing money into savings or money market accounts. If this is your financial institution's policy, deposit money in those accounts and transfer money to your checking account to cover checks.

$ Switch to another financial institution that charges lower fees for the products and services you use.

Foreign Exchange Fee: charge for converting a check denominated in a foreign currency into the local currency; generally $0—$20.00 per foreign check or draft; that's in addition to the potential differential in currency values. Suppose a Japanese businessman ordered a product and sent payment denominated in yen; the vendor would exchange the yen into US dollars or another appropriate currency.

$ Accept payment in your currency only. Let the customer bear the foreign exchange costs and risks. When you conduct business with foreign companies or customers, include a clause in the contract and invoice, that payment must be denominated in your local currency.

<u>Bad Deposit Fee</u>: a charge when you make a deposit and the payor's check or draft bounces. Your financial institution may charge $5.00—$20.00 per bounced check.

$ <u>Cash the check at the payor's (the person or company who issued the check) financial institution</u>. If you suspect a check will bounce, this tactic could help you avoid the bad deposit.

$ <u>Call the payor's financial institution to find out if the account balance is high enough to cover the check</u>. The call may help you avoid depositing a bad check but does not guarantee that your check will clear.   Although the account may have sufficient funds at the time of your call, another check may clear the payor's account, reducing the account balance below the amount of your check. If the payor's account balance is less than the amount of the check, don't deposit the check and contact the payor.

$ <u>Submit the check "For Collection"</u>. When you suspect a check may bounce, submit the check "for collection". Then your financial institution will send the check to the payor's financial institution who will hold the check until there are sufficient funds in his account to cover the check; however this does not guarantee that your check will be paid.

$ <u>Request cash or money orders</u>. Ask the payor to send payment via American Express® Moneygrams (1-800-543-4080) or Western Union (1-800-325-6000). Or, require US Postal Money Orders which are almost like cash.

$ <u>Request cashier's checks or certified checks</u>. These checks are considered more secure than personal checks because the financial institution pays the check. Cashier's Checks are drawn on the financial institution's own checking account. Your customer pays his financial institution which draws a check to you. When a financial institution certifies a check (Certified Check), they charge the payor's account for the amount of the check; this ensures the check will be paid.

<u>Check Printing Fee</u>: the charge to purchase a book of checks; generally $7.50—$20.00 per 200 checks.

$ <u>Buy checks from an outside vendor</u>. Even though financial institutions sell checks, you can purchase checks through the mail. An initial order of 200 personal checks cost almost $5.00 and 400 checks cost approximately $12.00. Call:

Company	Telephone Number
Checks in the Mail™	1-800-733-4443
Current® Check Printers	*1-800-533-3973*
Custom Direct Check Printers	1-800-272-5432

Choose the correct starting check number. And send the printer a voided check or the reorder form from your checkbook to make sure the following information appears on your checks: the correct account number, your name and address, and the financial institution's proper name. Before using the new checks, verify that your address and your financial institution's data are correct.

You can order duplicate checks which provide a carbon copy of each check, but if you keep record your financial transactions, duplicate checks should be unnecessary.

You can save more money by purchasing checks without the fancy designs or the leather checkbook.

$ <u>Choose a financial institution which offers free checks</u>. Some financial institutions offer free checks to customers who maintain certain minimum account balances or to attract new customers.

$ Open a checking account with your employer's commercial bank. The bank may offer company employees free checks. Contact your company's employee benefits department.

Stop Payment Fee: a fee charged when you wish to prevent a payee from depositing or cashing a check you have already written; generally $5.00—$15.00. You can request a stop payment order over the telephone, but you must deliver your request in writing to your financial institution before the check is presented to your financial institution for payment.

$ Mail checks only when you are certain you want to pay the bill. This should help you avoid having to place any stop orders on any checks.

$ Use credit cards. Often, a cardholder has 90 days in which to dispute credit card charges, and many credit card companies maintain helpful customer service departments to sort out disputed charges. Review your credit card company's policy.

FDIC Insurance Charge: charge to cover the financial institution's Federal Deposit Insurance Corporation's insurance premiums; not very common, but can be 25¢ per deposit or a percentage of your account balance.

$ Dispute the charge or choose a financial institution who doesn't assess this charge.

SUMMARY:
Analyze the services and products you need and purchase, and calculate the fees you incur for the services you use. You may be buying services you don't need and paying for products you don't use. Analyze the money savers outlined in this guide, and restructure your transactions and the way you manage your checking account. Then, you should reduce your checking account fees and save money.

3.   *THE BEST CHECKING ACCOUNT*
FOR YOU

Today, financial institutions offer a variety of products and
services under different brand names and at different prices (fees
and charges). Compare checking accounts carefully.

Jack wanted to select the checking account that best met his
needs, so we reviewed the following types of checking accounts.
Once you choose an account type, review chapters 2: Reduce
Your Checking Account Fees Now!, 4: Choose a Financial
Institution, and 8: Free or Not Free?.

Basic Checking Account: This account enables you to deposit
and withdraw money from your account and write checks.
Typically, there is no minimum balance requirement although
your financial institution charges a monthly account fee plus a
charge for each transaction one makes. With some accounts, the
monthly fee includes 6—10 free checks and 6—10 free ATM
uses. The monthly fee may also be stepped and when your
account balance exceeds certain levels, the monthly fee declines.
By law, these accounts don't usually pay interest income.

$ Use this account when you need a checking account and
cannot or choose not to meet the minimum or stepped balance
requirements for reduced fee or "Free Checking". Review
chapters 8: Free or Not Free? and 2: Reduce Your Checking
Account Fees Now!

Free Checking: This account requires you to maintain a certain
minimum deposit; and in exchange, you avoid ATM and per
check fees. Review chapter 2: Reduce Your Checking Account
Fees Now! and 8: Free or Not Free to determine whether a
"Free Checking" account can save you money.

NOW Accounts: NOW or "Negotiable Order of Withdrawal" is a "Free Checking" account that pays interest on your account balance. With NOW accounts, you earn interest on your money from the time your deposits become available as "cash" until the checks you write clear your account.

The minimum balance requirement for NOW accounts typically exceeds the minimum balance for "Free Checking", and the fees for dropping below the minimum balance can be high; however, you can earn more interest income every year — perhaps $50 or more.

$ Choose NOW accounts where the interest income is calculated on a day-of-deposit to day-of-withdrawal basis with daily compounding. This should maximize your interest income. Alternatively, when your financial institution pays interest on your month-end balance or lowest balance, you forfeit interest income because your financial institution pays interest on only part of your account balance.

$ Carefully analyze the actual interest rate you earn to determine whether a NOW account is cost-effective. For example, for different balances, Jack's financial institution might pay:

Average Daily Balance	Interest Rate
$0—$999	4.00%
$1,000—$1,999	4.25%
$2,000+	4.50%

$ Look for tiered or stepped interest rates whenever possible. With stepped rates, you receive higher interest rates based on higher account balances. If Jack's financial institution paid interest on stepped rates, when Jack's balance equalled $2,000 or more, he would earn 4.5% on his entire account balance.

Alternatively, under a blended rate, Jack would earn 4.00% on the first $999 on deposit; 4.25% on the next $1,000 on deposit; and 4.5% only on his balance in excess of $1,999.

$ If you have a "Free Checking" account and your account balance permanently falls below the minimum, change your account type or classification to a stepped fee account or basic checking account. This tactic may lower your overall fees.

$ Accelerate when your financial institution treats your deposits as "cash". Many financial institutions pay interest only on the "good funds" in your account — the amount of money in your account available as "cash". Review chapter 2: How to Reduce Checking Account Fees Now! for a description of the number of days it takes for a check to clear your account and tactics on how to accelerate when your deposits become available as "cash".

Super NOW Accounts: Super NOWs pay higher interest rates than NOW accounts. Super NOWs generally require higher minimum balances than NOWs. Depending on the differential between the interest rates on NOW and Super NOW accounts, the minimum balance requirement, and the rates of return you could earn from other investments, the NOW and Super NOW accounts may not be that worthwhile. To determine the impact of these factors on your particular situation, complete the cost-benefit analysis described in chapter 8: Free or Not Free.

Relationship, Cash Management, Asset Management, Priority, Packaged or Bundled Accounts: These accounts typically include checking and investment accounts, and credit cards, and often require higher balances. These accounts may charge an annual fee of $125—$250 and also charge for the products you purchase. For balances in excess of certain amounts, financial institutions often waive the fees. Brokerage houses, mutual funds, and commercial banks offer these accounts. These accounts can be convenient, and the financial institution may assign you a particular account officer or account representative who provides more personal service. But, you may save money by choosing the products and services you want and purchasing them separately, so it is important to compare prices.

Money Market Accounts With Check-Writing Privileges: Most financial institutions offer money market accounts with check-writing privileges. While you earn interest income on your balance until the checks clear, many money market accounts allow you to write only 3—6 checks per month or set high minimum per check amounts; as a result, these accounts may be impractical for paying monthly bills and withdrawing cash.

On the other hand, money market accounts typically pay interest rates that are higher than interest rates on day-to-day savings, NOW and Super NOW accounts. So, keep operating funds in your checking account to cover daily operating expenses, and emergency funds and short term savings in a money market account or mutual fund. Then, write checks to yourself or transfer money to your checking account as necessary.

In addition, you may be able to increase your rate of return and avoid depleting your savings by opening a money market account with a separate financial institution. Consider these mutual fund families which offer money market mutual funds with check-writing privileges:

Mutual Fund Family	Minimum Balance	Minimum Amount Per Check	Telephone Number
Janus Funds	$1,000	$250	1-800-525-8983
Twentieth Century Investors	$1,000	$500	1-800-345-2021
USAA	$1,000	$250	1-800-292-8706

<u>Credit Union Checking Accounts</u>: Credit unions are not-for-profit cooperatives organized to offer their members financial services at attractive prices.

Credit unions offer checking and savings accounts (both called share drafts), loans, Certificates of Deposit, mortgages, ATMs, credit and debit cards, Individual Retirement Accounts (IRAs), money orders and traveler's checks. Many credit unions insure deposits up to $100,000 with Federal Insurance (for example, the National Credit Union Administration). Be sure to join a credit union that's Federally insured.

Many companies, religious organizations, trade associations, and labor unions have organized credit unions. If you are ineligible to join your organizations' credit unions, to find a credit union you are eligible to join, contact the Credit Union National Association, Inc. (1-800-358-5710).

<u>SUMMARY</u>:
Generally, money market accounts are worthwhile for short term savings, but are inefficient for managing ongoing operating expenses and building wealth.

For most people, the basic checking account meets their needs because they need an account for writing checks and making cash withdrawals.

For other people, a "Free Checking" Account offers the most services and products at the most attractive fee structure, especially since many people tend to accumulate large balances in non-interest bearing or low-interest bearing accounts. Review chapter 8: Free or Not Free to analyze whether a "Free Checking" Account is economical for you.

4.   CHOOSE A FINANCIAL INSTITUTION

Today, people can open checking accounts with commercial banks, savings institutions, brokerage houses, mutual fund companies and credit unions. Once you have chosen the type of checking account that best meets your needs, choose a financial institution that offers you the products and services you want at the most attractive prices. Choose a financial institution for:

$ <u>Best combination of services, prices and fees for the products and services you want</u>. Financial institutions charge different fees and require different minimum balances for reduced fees. And interest rates on checking and savings accounts may vary across financial institutions.

$ <u>Safety</u>. Financial institutions vary by size and safety. At least once a year, check the safety of your financial institution with Veribanc, a banking research firm located in Boston (617-245-8370). Veribanc evaluates many insured financial institutions including banks, savings and loans, and credit unions. Order Veribanc's Blue Ribbon Bank Report (currently $38) which rates the top 35 banks in your region or one of their other research reports.

$ <u>Convenience</u>. Even though the national ATM networks enable people to maintain checking accounts with a financial institution based in another city, most people make the majority of their deposits and cash withdrawals near their home. Therefore, you may find it easier and more cost-effective to open a checking account with a financial institution located near your home, office, bus or train station.

$ <u>Relationship with your employer</u>. Many companies establish arrangements with their commercial bank where company employees can benefit from reduced fees or a "Free Checking" account. You can obtain direct deposit service where your employer deposits your payroll check directly into your checking account.

Many employers and trade associations sponsor credit unions who offer financial services at attractive prices. Review chapter 3: The Best Checking Account For You for more information on credit unions.

$ <u>Choose a financial institution that is Federally insured</u>. The Federal Deposit Insurance Corporation (FDIC) insures deposits in some but not all, banks and savings associations (see below). Federal Savings & Loan Insurance Corp. (FSLIC) insures deposits at some but not all savings and loan institutions. And many credit unions are insured by the National Credit Union Administration. Stick with financial institutions insured by Federally sponsored agencies instead of private insurers.

$ <u>NEVER EXCEED YOUR FINANCIAL INSTITUTION'S INSURANCE LIMITS</u>. Some financial institutions vary their deposit insurance, so find out your financial institution's policy now and restructure your accounts as appropriate.

<u>FDIC Insurance</u>:
FDIC deposit insurance protects deposits that are payable in the United States. **<u>Securities, mutual funds, and similar types of investments are not covered by deposit insurance</u>**.

Treasury bills, notes and bonds are not insured by Federal deposit insurance; however, they remain the property of the customer.

The FDIC insures deposits in different institutions separately. If an institution has many branches, a person's deposits in the main office and all branch offices are added together to determine the insurance coverage.

Deposits maintained in different categories of legal ownership are separately insured. Ownership is determined based on the "deposit account records". The most common types of accounts are single, joint, and testamentary (or trust) accounts.

Generally, each account type is insured up to the lesser of the deposits and $100,000.

IRA, Keogh, and "457 Plans" are insured separately from any non-retirement funds on deposit; but IRA and Keogh funds are added together and the combined total will be insured up to $100,000. Pension plans may face different rules so consult your plan's administrator.

Funds deposited by a corporation, partnership, or unincorporated association are insured up to a maximum of $100,000, and these deposits are insured separately from the personal accounts of the stockholders, partners or members. Funds owned by a sole proprietorship are treated as the individually owned funds of the sole proprietor.

Call the FDIC at 1-800-424-5488; or 202-898-3536 in Washington D.C. to request the book "Your Insured Deposit".

When your total deposits with any one financial institution exceed the financial institution's insurance coverage, remove the excess money and open accounts with other financial institutions.

The FDIC is considering reducing the insurance coverage from $100,000 to $50,000 so beware if the law changes and your deposits exceed the new insurance ceiling.

SUMMARY:
For most people, the optimal financial institution regarding a checking account is a commercial bank or their credit union. Choose a high quality credit union commercial bank that has many branches and ATMs located near your home; then managing your money should be relatively efficient. If your company or trade association offers a credit union, you might find that fees and charges for financial services are relatively inexpensive. For long term wealth-building, consider mutual funds. See chapter 11: Now You Don't.

5. SMART MONEY MANAGEMENT
Isolating Fees & Charges

Jack has found that the best way to discover how much he pays in fees and charges is to analyze several recent checking account statements. Periodically, Jack performs the following analysis to determine the nature and extent of his account charges. Then, he implements the strategies and tactics described in this guide to reduce his checking account fees.

<u>Obtain One or Two Recent Monthly Account Statements</u>. Jack happens to be a pack rat and saves all his checking account statements. But, if you haven't saved any recent statements, use your next two statements or request copies of two recent statements from your financial institution (only when there is no charge for the copies).

<u>Circle Every Account Charge on Your Statement. Then Verify Each Fee & Charge That Appears On Your Monthly Statement</u>. Your statement may itemize each charge or lump them together. If the fees and charges are not apparent, make a list of each charge and the corresponding amounts. Then contact the customer service department and request an explanation and calculation of each fee and charge.

<u>Add Up All the Other Charges</u>. Include the charges to your savings and money market accounts as well as your checking account. Total the fees and charges for several months; then calculate the average total fees; this is the total fees you incur every month and represents the typical monthly cost of maintaining your checking account.

You might be surprised to learn that your monthly charges total $25—$30. That equates to $300—$360 per year, in after-tax dollars. That might be a new outfit or two and certainly a few nice dinners.

An Example — Calculating Per Check Fees:
The following table illustrates how financial institutions charge
for checks you write. Suppose:
- Jack wrote 8 checks in March;
- 6 of the checks he wrote in March cleared his account in
  March; the other 2 checks Jack wrote in March cleared his
  account in April;
- he wrote 13 checks in April; only 11 cleared his account in
  April; the other 2 cleared his account in May or June.
- Jack's financial institution charges 25¢ per check that clears
  his account.

Financial institutions charge per check fees based on the number
of checks that clear your account during each statement period.
In March, six checks cleared Jack's account; at 25¢ each, Jack's
financial institution charged him $1.50 (25¢ multiplied by 6
checks) for writing checks:

Checks Cleared In:	Number of Checks	Per Check Charge	Monthly Charges
March	6	25¢	$1.50
April	13	25¢	$3.25
Later Months	2	25¢	50¢
Totals	21	—	$5.25

$ Once you identify all the charges to your account, change the
way you manage your money. Review chapters 2: Reduce
Your Checking Account Fees Now! and 3: The Best Checking
Account for You to lower your fees and save money.

Smart Money Management:
The key to saving money and building wealth is: **manage your
spending based on your calculation of your account balance,
not your financial institution's calculation**.

On any given day, your account balance in the financial institution's records is likely to exceed your account balance in your records. This difference arises because of the time lag between when you write checks and when they actually clear your account at your financial institution (outstanding checks).

Checks you write reduce your checkbook balance when you enter the transaction in your checkbook, but the financial institution adjusts your account balance only when the checks are presented for payment; several days or even weeks may pass between when you mail a check and when it clears your account (see chapter 2: Reduce Your Checking Account Fees Now! for information about when checks clear your account).

Similarly, your financial institution credits deposits to your account when they process them but your money may not become available as "cash" for several days until the deposits clear the payor's account. As a result, for deposits, your account records may show a greater available balance than your financial institution's records of your account.

When you manage your spending according to the financial institution's calculation of your account balance, you may spend more money than you have and bounce checks, resort to overdraft protection or run out of money. So monitor your account balance closely and adjust your spending accordingly.

$ <u>Write checks based on when your money becomes available as "cash"</u>. If Jack writes checks before his deposits become available as "cash", he may bounce those checks and incur heavy fees and charges, penalties and interest expense if the financial institution honors the check.

$ <u>Notice the timing difference between Jack's records and his financial institution's records</u>. When Jack paid his rent on March 2, he reduced his account balance by $450; however, the financial institution didn't know he paid the rent until March 9 when the check cleared his account. On March 2, there was $450 more in Jack's account according to his financial institution's records than per Jack's records. If Jack had followed the financial institution's accounting and spent more than $550 on March 2, the rent check would have bounced. Remember, base your spending on your account balance, not your financial institution's calculation.

Similarly, for account fees, your financial institution charges your account at the end of your statement month. And you may not know of the charges until you receive your monthly statement. As a result, for account fees and charges, your account balance per your records may exceed your balance according to the financial institution's records.

Account Balance Analysis:

Date	Transaction	Amount	Your Account Balance	Its Calcul- ation
3/1	Initial deposit	$1,000	$1,000	$1,000
3/2	Draw check to pay rent	$450	$550	$1,000
3/9	Rent check clears	$450	$550	$550
3/29	Account fees	$19	$550	$531

SUMMARY:

Determine how your financial institution charges your account and which products and services are subject to fees and charges.

First, enter all your transactions in your checkbook whenever you make a financial transaction. Second, keep your spending to an amount that's less than your account balance. Most important, manage your spending based on **your** account records, not your financial institution's records. Then you should avoid bouncing checks and never incur a deficit.

6. *BETTER MONEY MANAGEMENT*

Successful money management begins with a consistent money management system. This chapter explains the checkbook management program I have developed and used over the last ten years. The key is to adapt these methods to your personal finances in a way that your system is easy to use so you'll follow the system every month. Then you should attain your financial goals.

Save All Transaction Receipts. An accurate record keeping system begins with your financial transaction receipts for deposits, withdrawals and transfers. I store my receipts in an envelope until I reconcile my checking account. Jack even stores his receipts in chronological order which saves time when he reconciles his checkbook.

Save Your Canceled Checks. Generally, the IRS requires people to save tax-related items for the audit period or 7 years from the tax return's due date (April 15). Nonetheless, you may want to save them even longer, especially to determine the taxability of your retirement plan contributions and mutual fund investments.

Save your checkbooks and the individual canceled checks for at least 7 years. Canceled checks can help substantiate income tax deductions, and insurance and product warranty claims; and help you prove you paid disputed bills.

Buy a New Record Book Each Year. And Use a Different Record Book For Accounts With Each Financial Institution. I use one book to record the data for my accounts at each financial institution (checking, day-to-day savings, and money market accounts). I purchase a new record book every year to separate the financial transactions for different years because I find that the calendar year is a natural way to organize personal finances, especially since most people's personal income taxes coincide with a December 31 year-end.

Boxes of personal checks usually include a pocket-size record book or check register and my system can work with that check register. However, I prefer a larger book because I like to describe important transactions in greater detail. I understand that Jack keeps copious records too.

Consider National® Brand's books: the "Record Book" #56-401, and the "2-Column Book" #56-402. These books are available at stationery stores and are triple the size of a standard check register and provide more space to track your personal finances.

When you use the ledger book for keeping income tax records, the cost of the book should be tax-deductible under the Tax Act of 1986 (consult your accountant first).

Use Two Facing Pages to Record Your Checking Account Transactions. I start my checking account records at the beginning of the book and start my money market account and day-to-day savings account records in the middle of the book.

I linked my day-to-day savings and money market accounts to my checking account, so I can use my ATM card to transfer money between accounts easily. The money in my checking account funds daily operating expenses. My savings account warehouses money for near-term expenses, and I use my money market account to meet the minimum balance requirement for "Free Checking" and to accumulate enough money to meet the minimum investment for my mutual funds. For longer term savings, I prefer no-load mutual funds because there is no particular proof that load funds out perform no-load funds. **Separate accounts help me organize my money, segregate money for different purposes and avoid depleting my savings**.

Record Every Transaction. This is the most accurate way to track your finances. Once Jack got into the habit of recording his transactions when they took place, he found he needed only a few minutes each month to maintain his checkbook and he gained even greater control over his money.

Remember to record ATM withdrawals; checks you write; direct deposits such as payroll checks; debit card purchases; fees and charges; automatic payments; stop payments; voided checks; and money transfers between accounts.

For those checks you write at the office or the mall, enter the transactions in your checkbook when you get home. Jack carries a pen and index card in his pocket at all times to record his financial transactions and make other important notes. When Jack returns home, he copies the information from his index cards into his checkbook.

Keep a Running Balance in Your Checkbook. Never leave your checkbook without calculating the balance. When people postpone the calculations, they may spend too much money and bounce checks or drop below the minimum balance requirement and incur unnecessary fees. When you calculate your account balance after you make a transaction, you will know how much you can spend and should avoid running out of money.

$ The next two pages contain a sample checkbook ledger that shows how to manage your money with your checkbook.

1 Use five columns in your checkbook register to record your transactions.

Codes: Use codes and symbols to highlight important transactions so you can spot them easily when you need to prepare your income tax return and other financial documents. Always use the same symbol for a particular type of transaction you wish to track so your records will be consistent. Helpful codes include:

C charitable donations
D dividends (generally taxable)
E tax deductible or business expenses
I interest income from bonds
codes continued below the table on page 40.

Code	Date	Transaction
	3/1	Beginning Balance
	3/1	Direct Deposit - payroll
	3/1	Super Real Estate Co. - rent
	3/1	Cash withdrawal
	3/1	Interest Income (CI = $12.18)
	3/6	Payment to Credit Card
D	3/8	Deposit - XYZ Co. Dividend: $15
	3/8	Deposit - Gift Mom $100
	3/12	Void Check
(M)	3/15	Dr. Jeff (physical)
	3/16	Cash withdrawal
	3/28	Deposit (insurance reimbursement Dr. Jeff)
	3/29	The Mail House (500 address labels)
	3/31	Electric Company

Transaction codes continued from page 40.
   M medical expenses
   R revenue or income from freelance or business activities
   S savings
   T estimated income tax payments
   U non-reimbursed employee business expenses
   ★ use asterisks, arrows, circles or stars to flag other
      important transactions.

In the sample checkbook, in the code column, "D" highlights
the dividend income for income tax purposes, and "M" marks
the payment to Dr. Jeff as a medical expense.

		Amount	Balance
	✓	$0.00	$1,250.00
	✓	1,009.26	2,259.26
#136		<450.00>	1,809.26
	✓	<100.00>	1,709.26
	✓	4.36	1,713.62
#137	✓	<287.46>	1,426.16
	✓	0.00	1,426.16
	✓	115.00	1,541.16
#138	✓	0.00	1,541.16
#139		<85.00>	1,456.16
	✓	<50.00>	1,406.16
	✓	42.50	1,448.66
#140	✓	<6.37>	1,442.29
#141		<28.25>	1,414.04

<u>Date</u>: Record the date each transaction occurs.

<u>Transaction</u>: Describe transactions in detail to explain the transaction's purpose. Include enough information to describe the transaction and its significance in relation to income taxes and insurance — three or four words should be adequate. Notice the descriptions in the sample check register above.

Recently, Jack purchased address labels from a mail order company for the first time (check #140). In the "Transaction" column, he wrote the company's name along with the description "500 address labels". The description reminded him of the transaction purpose when he reconciled his checking account, enabled him to verify whether he had received the proper number of labels, and will help him compare prices for future orders.

Other helpful information to record is the terms of magazine, memberships, newsletter and newspaper subscriptions. By noting the expiration date of your subscriptions, you can verify how many issues you are entitled to receive and when it's renewal time.

For deposits containing several items, such as the dividend and the gift from mom in the example, use two lines to separate each transaction. Using two lines or two rows enables you to track and classify each transaction separately and spot mistakes — this is important for accurate record keeping.

Use checks in numerical order and record every check number in your checkbook. This should alert you to missing or lost checks or checks you may have written but never recorded.

When you put a check in your wallet, record the check number in your checkbook; this should remind you to record the transaction later or place a stop order on the check if you lose it. Jack uses the inside cover of his checkbook to sign out checks for this purpose; then he ✓'s them off after he enters the transaction in his checkbook.

Amount: Use this column to record the amount of each transaction. In the example, on March 1, Jack recorded $4.36 of interest income.

Balance: Use this column to calculate your account balance. I use a calculator because its math skills surpass mine and I find it helpful to perform the calculations twice to catch annoying mathematical errors.

2 Use brackets such as " < " and " > " to record transactions
   with negative numbers: amounts that should be subtracted
   from your account (cash withdrawals, checks you write, and
   fees and charges). Brackets help differentiate between positive
   and negative numbers and help you keep an accurate account
   balance. When you put a stop payment on a check, add back
   the amount of the check as a positive number and include the
   stop payment fee as a negative number in brackets.

3 CI stands for cumulative interest income. This helps track
   year-to-date interest income. Add each month's interest
   income to the prior month's cumulative interest. At year-end,
   CI should equal the interest income which appears on your
   Form 1099 (tax form) — this is the amount of interest income
   you should include in your income tax return.

4 Voided Checks. Occasionally you may write a check and
   decide to cancel it before giving it to the payee. Make an
   entry in your checkbook to void a check and track your
   checks in numerical sequence (check #138 in this example).
   Since the check was canceled, Jack entered $0.00 in the
   amount column because there was no change in cash position;
   and the account balance didn't change from the prior
   transaction.

   Mark the check "VOID" in large letters across the face of the
   check and tear out the signature block (the lower right hand
   corner); this way, no one can use the check. Keep the voided
   check with your canceled checks so your records will be
   complete.

$ Use symbols and marks to help you save money and
   simplify managing your money. In the example, when Jack
   paid Dr. Jeff, Jack drew an "M" in the code column to
   identify check #139 as a medical expense. When Jack
   received reimbursement from his insurance company, he
   drew a circle around the "M" to highlight that he received
   his benefits. The circle facilitates Jack's year-end analysis

43

(see chapter 12) and helps him verify that he received his insurance benefits.

If Jack hadn't received his health insurance benefits after three months, he would not have circled the "M" so he would have known he didn't receive reimbursement. Then he might resubmit his claim form.

$ <u>Link related transactions together with vertical lines</u>. Another way to gain more control over your money is to connect related financial transactions with vertical lines (see the medical expense). With the medical expense, the lines highlight that the particular reimbursement pertains to the payment to Dr. Jeff.

I use vertical lines for two types of transactions in addition to medical expenses. When I deposit money that is earmarked for a particular purpose, I link the deposit and the payment together. Second, when I deposit money that I want to save in my money market account, I use vertical lines to connect the deposit and the money transfer.

SUMMARY:
This chapter illustrated how to turn your checkbook into a valuable record keeping system and personal financial planning tool. Jack and I use codes and detailed descriptions to highlight and explain important transactions because the information helps us save taxes, organize our personal finances, and gain greater control over our money.

But, adapt this checkbook management system to your personal finances or develop your own system that works for you. Devise a system that is easy to use so your monthly effort will be minimal compared with the valuable information your checkbook provides and the money you save.

7.   BALANCING THE BOOKS
The Two Color System

With many people, years pass and they never reconcile their checkbook. They may find reconciling their checkbook to be a nuisance, especially after a long day at the office.

Why reconcile your checkbook?

There are several reasons: to gain more control over your money; to determine how much money you can spend; to ensure that your checks cleared your account for the correct amount; to catch mistakes early; to detect fraud and theft; to avoid bouncing checks; and to help you attain your financial goals.

What is an account reconciliation?

An account reconciliation compares the financial activity in your checkbook with the activity recorded on your monthly statement as computed by your financial institution. The objective of a reconciliation is to make both sets of account records reflect the same transactions and identify any open items.

1 Use Two Different Colors to Reconcile Your Checkbook. Under the Two Color System, I alternate colored pens because different colors facilitates my record keeping and helps differentiate transactions which cleared my account in different months. For transactions you made in January, make ✓'s in blue ink and for February activity, use a red or green pen, and alternate colors every month. Three or four colors might be better than two colors because checks that clear in different months might cause confusion if they are marked with the same color. Instead of using two colors, you could choose different symbols such as a "✓" and a "★".

Refer to the checkbook in Chapter 6 on pages 40—41.
Jack ✓'d each transaction that appeared on his March 29 statement to mark the transactions that cleared his account

according to both his and the financial institution's records. ✓s also help you make sure the same transaction doesn't clear your account twice.

Notice that Jack did not check off the payment to Dr. Jeff and the electric company (checks #139 & #141) because these checks did not clear his account in March; this means those transactions did not appear on Jack's monthly statement.

Financial institutions stagger individual checking account cycles throughout the month to maximize the usage of their data processing systems. Suppose Jack's checking account cycle ended on March 29. This means that transactions that cleared his account between February 28 and March 29 should appear on Jack's March 29 statement, and transactions that cleared his account after March 29, should appear on future statements, perhaps April or May.

Transactions which clear Jack's account after the March 29 statement cutoff date should appear on a subsequent statement. These items include deposits made after the close of business on the statement cutoff date or miscoded transactions which may result in a posting to someone else's account. Deposits should be posted to your account within two days (even though they may not become available as "cash" for several days), so if any deposits are missing from your statement, notify your financial institution and the payor immediately.

2 When You Receive Your Account Statement, Enter Any New Items In Your Checkbook. Such entries include interest income, fees and charges. Verify that the charges are consistent with your financial institution's fee schedule. Mark the transaction column ("✓" or "★") since these items cleared your account per your financial institution's records.

3 Put Your Canceled Checks In Numerical Order. This should simplify the reconciliation because your account statement probably lists canceled checks in numerical order.

4 <u>For Each Canceled Check, Make a ✓ in the Transaction Column.</u>

When checks clear your account (canceled checks), the financial institution generally prints the amount which they charged your account in the lower right hand corner of the check. You can verify that the amount of the check equals the amount printed in the lower right hand corner (for example, that the check cleared your account for the proper amount). If the two amounts don't equal, notify your financial institution as soon as possible to correct the error.

If any transactions erroneously appear on your statement, notify your financial institution immediately. This activity could result from an error or fraud.

Occasionally, a check will clear your account but may not be returned to you. If the check appears on your statement, mark it as cleared in your checkbook. Your financial institution can send you a copy of the check (free of charge).

<u>Checks older than six months generally cannot be cashed.</u> Sometimes a check may get lost or the payee won't cash it. After a few months, if you suspect that the check will not be deposited, "★" or circle the transaction in your checkbook and place a stop payment on the check. In the current month, make an adjusting entry to add back the amount and correct your balance. In the description column, note the original check number so you can locate the related check in the event the check is recovered and clears your account.

Financial institutions honor checks that are less than six months old if the signatures on the check match the signature card in the financial institution's files and there are sufficient funds in the person's account to cover the check. Checks from the US Treasury, however, are valid indefinitely. Try to deposit checks as soon as you receive them. And void checks that are outstanding for more than six months.

5 <u>Put Transaction Receipts in Chronological Order</u>. For each deposit, withdrawal, and transfer that appears on your account statement, make a ✓ in the transaction column. The date printed on the ATM receipt should be the date you executed the transaction but may differ from the date per your statement because the financial institution may update its records the following day or on Monday for weekend transactions. ✓ only those transactions that appear on that month's statement.

Once you have verified all your transactions and the account reconciliation works, if you like, discard the transaction receipts for that month's activity. Store the remaining ATM receipts in your receipts file or in your checkbook for future months' reconciliations. Keep your account statements for at least one year to maintain complete records.

Jack ✓'s or circles each ATM transaction on his account statement as well as in his checkbook to ensure that he has recorded all of the transactions in his checkbook which clear his account and appear on his monthly statement.

6 <u>Reconcile Your Checking Account EASILY</u>. After you have ✓'d every transaction that appears on your statement, your checkbook and account statement should reflect the same information expect for the unmarked items which should be transactions that have not cleared your account.

The most common reconciling item is outstanding checks which are checks you wrote but have not cleared your account. Due to outstanding checks, usually, the ending balance on your monthly statement will exceed your balance calculation. To reconcile your account, reverse each open transaction (unmarked) in your checkbook: add back those items that were originally subtracted from your balance (for example, checks and withdrawals) and subtract those items that were originally added to your balance (for example, deposits and interest income).

In the example, the ending balance per Jack's checking account statement equals $1,977.29. Jack scanned his checkbook and focused on the last transaction he ✓'d off: check #140. Jack turned on his calculator and entered his checkbook account balance which corresponds to the last marked transaction: $1,442.29. This is the first entry Jack used to reconcile his checkbook.

Jack's Account Reconciliation

Transaction	Amount
Balance for reconciliation	$1,442.29
Outstanding Check #139	$85.00
Outstanding Check #136	$450.00
Reconciled balance	$1,977.29

Then, Jack reversed (added or subtracted) each transaction which was not ✓'d off: checks #139 and #136. The remaining transactions which occurred after the statement closing date (March 29) that are not ✓'d off (check #141) should not have cleared Jack's account in March and should be ignored for the March reconciliation.

Jack's March reconciliation calculation would be: $1,442.29 plus $85 plus $450, which equals $1,977.29 (the ending balance per the account statement).

Next month, Jack would alternate symbols and use a "★" or use a different colored pen to reconcile his account.

$ $ $

What Happens IF The Reconciliation Doesn't Work???

1 Check your math. Even with a calculator, I have entered numbers incorrectly. Recalculate the running balance in your checkbook. You may find a math error. Enter the amount as an error and calculate the correct balance.

2 Make sure you posted all of the transactions correctly, especially transfers between accounts and automatic payments. Also, make sure you ✓'d off each transaction that cleared your account. Compute an account balance and try to reconcile your account again.

3 Reconcile your checkbook and calculate the difference between your calculated checkbook balance and the ending balance that appears on your statement.

Look for transposition errors. If the difference between the sum of your account balance and reconciling items, and your ending balance per your statement is evenly divisible by 9, you may have switched the order of the numbers you added to or subtracted from your balance. For example, if Jack's calculated account balance was $1442.29 and for check #139 he added 58 instead of adding 85, the difference of 27 (85 minus 58) is divisible by 9.

Look for doubling errors. If the difference as illustrated above is divisible by 2 with no remainder, Jack probably added a number that should have been subtracted from his account balance, or subtracted a number that should have been added to his balance.

If you locate the error, adjust your checkbook balance and repeat the account reconciliation.

4 If steps #1, #2, and #3 fail, repeat step #2 and make sure you recorded all your transactions. Then, reconcile your checkbook under the Two Color Method and ✓ off all of the transactions which appear in your checkbook and on your statement. Calculate the difference between the calculated checkbook balance in your reconciliation and the balance on your account statement. Enter that amount in the transaction column as an adjustment. Don't worry about the difference.

8.   *FREE OR NOT FREE?*

"Free Checking" accounts include a checking account without the fees and charges. The concept of "Free Checking", however, is confusing because financial institutions who offer "Free Checking" generally require a minimum account balance. The minimum balance represents an opportunity cost to you because you could invest the money elsewhere. But, the important question is whether "Free Checking" saves you money. And this chapter illustrates how you can determine whether "Free Checking" saves you money.

<u>What is your financial institution's minimum balance requirement for "Free Checking"</u>? Minimum balances for "Free Checking" can range from $1,500—$6,000. Before performing any calculations, find out if your employer sponsors a credit union or has an arrangement with its commercial bank to offer company employees reduced fee or "Free Checking".

<u>How is your minimum balance calculated?</u> The average daily account balance is the most beneficial method: your financial institution calculates your average daily balance each month, and when your average daily balance exceeds the required minimum, the financial institution waives the fees.

Other financial institutions set a minimum dollar balance and even when your account balance drops below the minimum for only one day, you pay the fees.

Often, your deposits must become available as "cash" in your account to be counted towards the minimum balance. See chapter 2: Reduce Your Checking Account Fees Now!

<u>Which account balances count towards the minimum balance requirement</u>? To determine whether you meet the minimum balance, many financial institutions include balances in the following accounts: CDs, checking, NOW, Super Now, savings, money market, and IRAs.

$ Ignore your checking account balance to meet the minimum balance requirement. Since checking account balances tend to fluctuate widely throughout the month, your checking account balance may inadvertently drop below the minimum balance and you might incur extra fees and charges.

$ Analyze your IRA investments carefully: To count IRA balances towards the minimum balance requirement for "Free Checking", your financial institution may require you to invest in savings or money market accounts or CDs.

Traditionally, over the long run, the returns on CDs and money market accounts have been lower than rates of return on other investments. Especially if you are at least ten years away from using the money, consider investing a portion of your portfolio in several high quality, diversified no-load common stock mutual funds. But, consult your investment adviser before making or changing your investments.

$ Keep your money in the account that offers the highest interest rate and the lowest risk. For short-term savings, this may be a money market account, money market mutual fund, or CD. Money market accounts allow you to make daily withdrawals while the maturities of CDs range from 3 months to 5 years. When you break a CD prior to maturity, the financial institution charges you a penalty. If you choose a long term CD, make sure you won't need the money before maturity. Or, open several CDs including both short and long maturities.

Determine the interest income you would earn by choosing "Free Checking". Estimate your average daily balance or the amount of money which qualifies for interest income. To perform an accurate analysis, treat each account separately, especially when the interest rates are different.

1 Suppose Jack's financial institution permits him to invest the $2,000 minimum balance requirement as follows:

After-Tax Income Calculation Table:

Account	Amount	Interest Rate	Annual Interest Income	After-Tax Income (30% rate)
Checking	$500	0.00%	$0.00	$0.00
CD	$1,500	5.00%	$75.00	$52.50
Savings	$0	2.00%	$0.00	$0.00
Money Market	$0	4.00%	$0.00	$0.00
IRA	$0	4.25%	$0.00	$0.00
Totals	$2,000	—	$75.00	$52.50

Jack's financial institution pays 0% interest on checking account balances, and 5% on CDs. In this example, Jack's financial institution requires him to leave $500 on deposit in his checking account so his checking account balance cannot fall below $500.

Each account appears on a different line in the table with the balance and interest rate. If the interest rates change or other accounts qualify towards the minimum balance, Jack would adjust his analysis accordingly.

2 Convert all interest income figures to after-tax amounts to compare the costs and benefits of "Free Checking". Uncle Sam charges income taxes on interest income, and we pay personal checking account fees and charges in after-tax dollars which means there is no tax deduction. Convert all amounts into after-tax dollars:

Pre-Tax Interest Income multiplied by
(1 minus tax rate)

Jack earns $75 in pre-tax interest income from his CD, and at a combined Federal, state and local tax rate of 30%, he pays $22.50 ($75 multiplied by the tax rate or 30%) in income taxes. His after-tax interest income is $52.50 ($75 multiplied by 70% or 100%—30%).

3 <u>Estimate your annual account fees and charges</u>. Jack pays $20 per month in fees and charges. Annual fees equal $240 every year ($20 multiplied by 12 months).

Average Total Monthly Fees
multiplied by 12

4 <u>Calculate how much investment income you forfeit with the "Free Checking" account?</u> Often, interest rates on checking and day-to-day savings accounts are lower than the returns from money market accounts or mutual funds. With "Free Checking", Jack's minimum balance is $2,000 so he forfeits the opportunity to invest the $2,000 in an investment, for example, that bears the same degree of risk and pays 7%. Therefore, Jack loses pre-tax investment income of $140 (7% return multiplied by $2,000 investment). Pre-tax income of $140 equals $98 after-tax ($140 multiplied by 100%—tax rate, or $140 multiplied by 100%—30% or 70%).

5 <u>Complete your own cost-benefit analysis to determine whether "Free Checking" saves you money</u>. See the results of Jack's cost-benefit analysis on the next page.

For Jack, "Free Checking" saves him $194.50, after-tax, this year. If Jack could make a $2,000 investment bearing the same degree of risk and earn a rate of return greater than 7%, then the opportunity cost (lost income) of "Free Checking" would exceed $98. The cost of "Free Checking" varies across financial institutions depending on the rates of return on alternative investments and the minimum balance requirement for a "Free Checking" account. Shop around for the best deal and perform your own cost-benefit analysis.

The Results of Jack's Cost-Benefit Analysis:

Benefits from "Free Checking":	Amount
After-tax interest income:	$52.50
After-tax fees and charges saved:	$240.00
Other:	$0.00
Total Gains:	$292.50

Costs with "Free Checking":	
After-tax income from other investments forfeited:	< $98.00 >
Other:	$0.00
Total Losses:	< $98.00 >
After-Tax Gain or < Loss > from "Free Checking":	$194.50

$ <u>Consider switching to "Free Checking" if you have accumulated large balances in low or non-interest bearing accounts.</u> Review your account statements and your financial institution's requirements for "Free Checking" because you might already qualify for "Free Checking".

SUMMARY:
Perform the cost-benefit analysis illustrated in this chapter to determine whether "Free Checking" will save you money. If you typically accumulate large balances in low-interest or non-interest bearing accounts, you may save money by switching to a "Free Checking" account.

Depending on your investment objectives and your investment horizon, over the long run, you may be able to achieve higher returns by choosing alternative investments such as high quality, no-load diversified mutual funds comprised of common stocks and investment-grade corporate bonds; but consult your investment adviser before changing your investment portfolio.

9.   *USE YOUR CHECKBOOK AS A FINANCIAL PLANNING TOOL*

Many people consider a personal checkbook to be merely a record of cash inflows and outflows. I find that when I keep my checkbook up-to-date, it provides extensive information about my financial health and becomes a valuable personal financial planning tool.

This chapter explains how to set up your checkbook as a financial planning tool.

Record All Your Financial Activity In Your Checkbook. Make sure you have recorded all your transactions in your checkbook. If you have not kept a checkbook before, you can start at any time (review chapter 14: Chaotic Records). Or, use a recent account statement for a month which represents your typical spending habits.

Review Your Checkbook to See How You Spend Your Money. Look for excessive credit card spending, large and frequent cash withdrawals and payments for unnecessary purchases (out-of-pocket spending). Once you take note of how you spend your money, change your spending habits to save money and attain your financial goals.

Create your own Monthly Cash Flow Calculator (as illustrated on page 59) to calculate how much money you can spend without incurring a deficit.

Isolate the Transactions For One Month By Drawing Two Horizontal Lines. Choose one typical month. Draw a horizontal line above the first transaction of the month, and draw a second horizontal line below the last transaction which occurs in the month you are analyzing.

$ $ $

Circle Monthly Take-Home-Pay With a Green Pen. To calculate your monthly take-home-pay accurately, include only the number of paychecks you receive in any given month. If you get paid once or twice a month or once a week, it should be relatively easy to calculate your monthly take-home-pay (although your take-home-pay may change when you meet certain thresholds such as social security tax).

Monthly take-home-pay equals:

> Amount of each paycheck multiplied by
> the number of paychecks per year,
> divided by 12

$ **Monthly take-home-pay should become your monthly spending ceiling.** When you spend your take-home-pay or less, you should avoid running a deficit. For more strategies on budgeting, saving and investing money, obtain my book the Personal Budget Planner — A Guide for Financial Success at your public library or local bookstore, or photocopy the order form on page 96 of this guide.

$ **If Monthly Net Cash Flow is less than zero, you are spending too much money.** Cut your credit card and out-of-pocket spending. If you typically run out of money before the next pay period, your spending may be too high.

Circle **Fixed Costs** With a Red Pen. Fixed costs are costs people incur every month regardless of their activities, and in the short term, fixed costs don't change in amount. Fixed costs include rent, mortgage, and condominium maintenance payments; loan payments, car payments, commuting costs, utility payments (electricity, telephone, gas and oil); and automatic monthly investments (see chapter 11: Now You Don't). Total your fixed costs and set aside enough money to pay these expenses every month.

Circle **Periodic Costs** With a Blue Pen. People incur periodic costs throughout the year but at different times during the year. Periodic costs include insurance premiums, medical expenses, automobile repair bills, club dues, estimated income tax payments, and vacation costs. While these costs are not as rigid as fixed costs, periodic expenses remain relatively constant from year to year, so you should be able to estimate these costs.

$ Set aside some money for periodic expenses every month. Estimate your annual periodic costs and set aside 1/12th of your annual periodic expenses every month. This should help you save enough money to pay these bills when they come due. For vacations in particular, this strategy can help you avoid costly credit card debt. When you implement this tactic, keep the money in a high quality money market account or money market mutual fund to earn interest income; the objective is to accumulate money to pay bills in the near term, not assume greater risk to earn the highest rate of return.

Total Outflows for Personal Spending. These include cash withdrawals, credit card spending and other payments. Many account statements total monthly cash withdrawals. If not, circle each cash withdrawal in your checkbook and calculate the total.

$ Limit personal spending to less than your monthly take-home-pay minus fixed costs minus 1/12 of your annual periodic costs. This should help you avoid running a deficit. Every few months, perform this calculation and when you spend more than this amount, lock up your checkbook.

$ Track your out-of-pocket spending for one or two months. Many people have difficulty controlling their out-of-pocket spending; once they withdraw cash, the money disappears. Make a list of every expenditure you make; then adjust your spending to fit within your income and expense structure. Don't resort to extra cash withdrawals or cash advances on credit cards; instead, cut your spending.

$ Lock your credit cards in a drawer for several months. Review chapter 10: Now You See It for strategies about managing credit cards.

$ To avoid deficits, project your income and expenses and set your spending. Start with your checking account balance and add projected deposits, fixed and periodic costs. The remaining balance equals the amount you can spend without incurring a deficit. If your calculated balance is less than zero, you may bounce checks or run out of money.

Monthly Cash Flow Calculator (example):

Category	Amount
Total Monthly Take-Home-Pay	$1,700
Monthly Fixed Costs	<$900>
Monthly Periodic Cost Savings	<$100>
Monthly Credit Card Payments	<$560>
Monthly Cash Withdrawals	<$800>
Other Checks Paid	<$0>
Monthly Net Cash Flow	<$660>

In this example, Jack's Monthly Net Cash Flow is less than zero which means his spending and expenses exceed his income. He risks bouncing checks or having to borrow from lines of credit, overdraft protection, or credit cards. Jack should analyze his costs and spending and make cuts to avoid incurring deficits.

Monthly Net Cash Flow should always be greater than zero, except when you incur periodic costs, go on vacation, or face an emergency which requires increased spending. Even then, you can usually prepare for unexpected expenses by setting aside money in advance.

10. *NOW YOU SEE IT*

Your checkbook contains symptoms of financial health just as a doctor's physical examination reveals symptoms of illness. Review your checkbook and if the items described in this chapter appear, they are symptoms of poor financial health — you may be wasting money or missing opportunities to build wealth. When these items appear in your checkbook, implement the strategies and tactics described below to improve your financial health, save more money and build more wealth.

When you finish implementing the techniques explained in this chapter, review the next chapter, Now You Don't (See It) which highlights transactions that should appear in your checkbook to help you build wealth.

High Checking Account Balances.   Unfortunately, too many people accumulate large balances in checking and savings accounts which pay little or no interest. This means they forfeit interest income.   Keep your checking account balance high enough to cover your checks and spending, and keep the extra money in interest-bearing accounts. For longer term savings and wealth-building, choose high quality no-load mutual funds which invest in common stocks and bonds, but consult your investment adviser before changing your portfolio.

When you link all your accounts to your checking account, with your ATM card, it is easy to transfer money from interest-bearing accounts to your checking account to cover checks. This tactic requires extra effort and more accurate record keeping, but should increase your interest income every year.

Ending Account Balance Less Than Beginning Account Balance. This means your spending exceeds your income. Reduce your spending and expenses until your total cash outflow is less than your take-home-pay or until your ending account balance is greater than or equal to your beginning balance.

Bounced Check Fees Occur Frequently or You Have a Negative Checking Account Balance. This means you are spending too much money. Lock up your checkbook. Make a spending plan and cut your spending to the necessities until you return to financial health.

More Than 3 Cash Withdrawals Per Week. In addition to incurring excess ATM fees, if you are making more than three cash withdrawals per week, your spending may exceed your weekly cash budget. Make only one ATM cash withdrawal every week. This should reduce your ATM fees and help you manage your out-of-pocket spending. Keep your spending to your weekly cash budget or less, and when you run low on cash, stop spending money.

Income Tax Refund Exceeds $1,000. This means you have made an interest-free loan to Uncle Sam. Raise your personal exemptions to increase your take-home-pay, but use the extra money to reduce your credit card debt or open an investment account to build more wealth.

Excessive Income Tax Payments. Estimated tax payments may be a function of under-withholding of income taxes or business or investment income which was not subject to withholding. To reduce your income taxes, consider increasing tax-deductible contributions to retirement plans, buying a home, and investing in municipal or government securities. And, hire an accountant.

Deposits For Capital Gains, Dividends, or Interest Income From Stocks, Bonds or Mutual Funds. To maximize your wealth, reinvest all income, dividends, and distributions in the fund. If you currently receive distributions from your mutual funds, switch to "automatic reinvestment" which enables you to purchase more shares in the fund and take advantage of compound returns. If you receive income checks from stocks or bonds, after the checks clear, send a check for the same amount back to your mutual fund or investment account or open a new mutual fund account to diversify your portfolio.

Frequent Money Transfers or Withdrawals from Savings Accounts to Fund Spending. You may be depleting your savings. Reduce your spending and open a savings, money market, or mutual fund account with a separate financial institution to preserve your wealth. Then, keep only enough money in your savings and checking accounts to fund operating expenses and maintain a cushion for unforeseen expenses. Deposit your extra money with the other financial institution.

Total Monthly Debt Payments Exceed 36% of Income. Many bankers use this rule of thumb to evaluate a borrower's capacity to repay a loan. When your total debt payments exceed 36% of your income, reduce your spending and repay as much debt as possible, especially high-cost credit card debt.

[Credit Card Debt Plus Out-of-Pocket Spending] Exceeds 75% of [Take-Home-Pay Minus Fixed Costs]. This means you may not be saving enough money to cover periodic expenses such as quarterly estimated income tax payments, insurance premiums, vacation costs, medical costs and automobile repairs. Also, you may not be saving enough money for the future.

Frequent Cash Advances on Credit Cards. Your spending may exceed your take-home-pay. Reduce your spending, consider taking a second job, and use the extra money to reduce your credit card debt. This can be a sign that your spending is too high and you are incurring costly credit card interest.

Excessive Payments to Service Consumer Debt. Four signs of excessive spending are: the existence of credit card debt; where the monthly credit card payment equals the minimum payment; average monthly credit card bill exceeds 15% of take-home-pay; or you cannot pay off your credit card bill in full. Most people use consumer debt to fuel personal spending and current consumption, but consumer debt limits wealth-building. First, consumer debt generally carries costly interest expense. Second, when you continually make only the minimum payment, at a 20% rate of interest, your debt doubles almost every four years.

62

$ Make extra payments on consumer loans and credit card debt. Pay off high-cost debt as quickly as possible, especially when extra payments reduce your principal. For some consumer loans, the financial institution treats excess payments as advance payments of future months' installments and not reductions of the loan balance; then advance payments won't reduce your interest expense.

$ Stop using your credit cards until you pay off the debt. Make payments to your credit cards when you receive your paycheck; don't wait for the next due date. Extra payments reduce your outstanding balance which lowers your interest expense. Then, leave your credit cards in a drawer until you pay off all your credit card debt and cancel all but two or three cards. Going forward, keep your credit card spending to an amount you can pay off in full. If you cannot use credit cards without incurring debt, leave them at home or use cash.

$ Switch to a credit card which charges a lower interest rate. Every month, Money® magazine (1-800-336-0079) lists credit cards with low interest rates. In most cases, it is advantageous to choose a card which offers a grace period.

$ Retire high interest rate debt with secured debt. Secured debt such as passbook loans, auto loans and home-equity loans usually carry lower interest rates than unsecured consumer debt because secured debt is supported by collateral. Once you refinance high interest rate debt, cut your spending and don't incur new consumer debt.

$ Take out a home-equity loan. Under the current tax law, in most cases, the interest on home-equity loans up to $100,000 in principal is tax-deductible. If you take out a home-equity loan to pay off high-cost credit card debt and incur more consumer debt, you may double the amount you owe. If you default on a home-equity loan, the lender may seize your home to pay off the loan.

Monthly Payments to More Than Three Credit Cards. For most of us, two or three credit cards should provide plenty of credit. When you maintain more than three credit cards, you may be paying unnecessary annual fees and heavy interest charges.

$ Cancel extra credit cards. I use one credit card for personal expenses and one credit card for business expenses. This simplifies my record keeping, helps me separate business and personal expenses, and makes it easier to submit expense reports to my employer. My wife keeps a credit card in her own name so she continues to build her own credit rating.

Payments to Store or House Credit Cards. Many retailers issue their own credit cards although most of them accept Visa and Mastercard. Consolidate your credit cards into one or two major credit cards. This should reduce the number of checks you write and highlight how much you spend every month.

Payments for Small Amounts. This raises per check fees and the postage bill. Review chapter 2: Reduce Your Checking Account Fees Now!

Outstanding Balance On Overdraft Protection For More Than Two Consecutive Months. Ideally, overdraft protection should be used as a safety net to fund short-term cash crunches and avoid bouncing checks, not to fuel spending or meet long term financing needs. When you draw on overdraft protection, cut your spending and pay down consumer debt starting with the loan with the highest interest rate.

Monthly Housing Costs Exceed 25%—50% of Monthly Income. This ratio is a range because the cost of housing varies by area. Regardless of where you live, when housing costs strain your spending, consider moving to a less expensive home, sharing an apartment, refinancing your mortgage, or renting out a room, the garage or storage space (research your homeowner's insurance policy carefully and hire a competent lawyer to draft a lease).

Monthly Loan Payments for Appliances and Consumer Goods. For major purchases such as a washing machine, refrigerator, or an automobile, it may be necessary to borrow money to make the purchase. This is okay; however, remember that the interest expense raises the cost of the appliance.

$ Save money ahead of time. At least six months before the intended purchase date, every month, deposit money in a low-risk, money market account or money market mutual fund. This should reduce your borrowing and interest expense.

$ Shop around for the best consumer loan. Interest rates on consumer loans vary across financial institutions. The store credit company's loan may not be the lowest interest rate available. Contact several financial institutions, your credit union, your insurance agent and your commercial bank.

$ Make extra payments to reduce consumer loans. For most loans, payments in excess of the monthly amount reduce your principal balance, and extra payments will reduce your interest expense. Most credit companies, however, require borrowers to make a minimum payment every month regardless of any extra payments they make so monitor your spending closely.

$ Ignore the credit company's monthly payment book. Credit companies typically send borrowers a payment book which contains monthly coupons. The payment may be a small amount designed to stretch out the loan and maximize the credit company's interest income. Typically, extra payments will reduce your loan balance. Especially for relatively inexpensive items such as personal stereos, the interest expense can substantially increase the cost of the appliance.

Excessive Insurance Premiums. Some people buy insurance coverage they don't need. One example is life insurance when they have no heirs or dependents. When you switch to a new insurance policy, receive the insurance certificates from the new policy before canceling your existing insurance policy.

Two other expensive insurance policies are credit life insurance and mortgage or loan life insurance which pay your loan balance in the event you die. Generally, it is less expensive to purchase term life insurance which provides benefits upon your death.

Typically, you can lower your insurance premiums by raising your deductible which is the amount of loss you bear before you become eligible for proceeds from your insurance company.

Home Mortgage Interest Rate Exceeds Market Rates by 2% or More. You might be able to refinance your mortgage at lower market rates and save thousands of dollars. For refinancing to be cost-effective, make sure you will recover the up-front fees within the number of years you plan to live in your home; generally, 2—3 years. If you have an adjustable rate mortgage (ARM) and market mortgage rates are at a cyclical low, you may want to lock in a fixed interest rate or switch to a 30-year fixed rate mortgage to lock in the low interest rates.

Insurance Premiums for Collision Damage on Old Automobiles. The cost of this coverage may exceed the value of your car. Visit your auto mechanic, insurance agent or public library to determine the "blue book" value of your car. When the cost of the collision damage coverage exceeds the value of the car, consider dropping the coverage. However, when you cancel the collision damage coverage and get in an accident, you will have to pay for any repairs yourself — this is called self-insurance.

Excessive and Frequent Payments for Automobile Repairs. It may be time to trade in your old car.

Monthly Utility Payments Exceed $50. Install insulation in your house and turn off appliances and lights when you leave your home. In the winter, turn down the thermostat and wear sweaters. In the summer, turn down the air conditioner and wear shorts. If your home has electric heat, consider switching to natural gas or oil. Contact your utility to learn more ways to reduce your energy costs and conduct a home energy audit.

Monthly Telephone Bills Exceed $50.

$ Make calls during discount calling periods. These times usually include: weekdays before 8am and after 11am; all day Saturday; and Sunday before 5pm and after 11pm.

Take advantage of different time zones. When you place calls from New York to California, call after 11pm and you will pay at the discount rate.

$ Switch to another long distance telephone service to reduce your long distance telephone bill. Different carriers may offer lower rates to your most frequent calling areas: ATT (1-800-225-5288); MCI® (1-800-444-4444); Metromedia® (1-800-275-0200); and Sprint® (1-800-877-4646).

Many Payments to Cable Television Shopping Shows and Mail Order Catalogs. You may be incurring costly credit card debt or spending money that you could be investing for the future.

High Monthly Payments to Cable Television Services. Your subscription package may include channels you rarely watch. Compare the channels you receive with the channels you watch and scale back your service to a less expensive package which includes your favorite channels.

SUMMARY:
So, Now You See It. This chapter described transactions which can be symptomatic of financial trouble. Every year, scan your checkbook for the items described in this chapter. If the transactions described in this chapter appear in your checkbook, eliminate them to improve your financial position. Then, you will save more money and build more wealth.

The next chapter, Now You Don't (See It) describes transactions which should appear in your checkbook — transactions that are symptomatic of financial health.

11. NOW YOU DON'T
(SEE IT)

Your checkbook contains symptoms of financial health just as a doctor's physical examination reveals symptoms of illness. This chapter describes transactions which are symptomatic of financial health — transactions that should appear in your checkbook. Review your checkbook and account statements, and when these items don't appear in your records, you may be wasting money or missing opportunities to build wealth. Then, implement the following strategies and tactics to improve your financial health, save more money and build more wealth.

If you haven't reviewed the previous chapter, Now You See It, turn back now.

No Automatic Monthly Investment Program. Most mutual fund families offer these programs where they transfer a fixed sum of money from your checking account to your mutual fund account every month, free of charge. Automatic monthly investment transfers offer no-excuses saving. You save money every month, and your money works for you continuously.

Consider these two mutual fund families which have no initial minimum account balances:

Mutual Fund Family	Minimum Monthly Investment	Telephone Number
Janus Funds	$50	1-800-525-8983
Twentieth Century Investors	$25	1-800-345-2021

To find out about other mutual funds, obtain the following publications:

Magazine or Publication	Telephone Number
Business Week	1-800-635-1200
Forbes	1-800-888-9896
Money®	1-800-336-0079
Morningstar Mutual Funds	1-800-876-5005
Smart Money	1-800-444-4204

No Contributions to Retirement Plans. Unfortunately, more and more companies are reducing pension plan and post-retirement medical benefits, and social security payments do not seem to cover all of our retirement needs. Therefore, it is crucial for us to save money for our retirement.

The most powerful way to prepare for retirement is to establish a 401(k) plan, 403(b) plan or IRA; and if you are self-employed, open a Keogh Plan or SEP IRA (Simplified Employee Pension IRA). Qualified contributions to retirement accounts reduce your taxable income in the year of contribution, and the income accumulates tax-free until you make withdrawals.

There are limits to contributions and penalties associated with withdrawals before you reach age 59½; and withdrawals become mandatory at age 70½; so consult your accountant before opening such accounts and making contributions or withdrawals.

No Contributions to a Spousal IRA. Typically, a non-working spouse can contribute up to $250 to an IRA and deduct the contribution on the couple's tax return. Consult your accountant before taking action.

No Contributions to a Non-Deductible IRA. Every year, individuals can make contributions to their IRAs equal to the lower of their earned income and $2,000; even if they are covered by a qualified pension plan.

The contribution's tax deductibility depends on whether the person participates in a qualified retirement or pension plan (for example 401(k) or 403(b) plan) and his earned (salary) income. Under non-deductible or Form 8606 IRAs, contributions are in after-tax dollars, but the income accumulates tax-free until withdrawal. There are restrictions and penalties associated with these IRAs, so consult your accountant before taking action.

No Payments for IRA Custodian Fees. Many IRA custodians charge annual fees of $10. If you receive a bill for the fee and don't pay the fee by the due date, the custodian deducts the fee from your account. This reduces your retirement plan assets. Even though a $10 annual deduction may seem insignificant, it is more advantageous to write a check for the annual fees and keep the maximum amount of money working for you.

No Savings for Periodic Expenses. Since periodic expenses occur at different times throughout the year, it is important to save enough money to meet these expenses. See chapter 9: Use Your Checkbook As A Financial Planning Tool.

No Direct Deposits. Sign up for direct deposit service for paychecks, social security and pension payments and other monthly income payments. Under direct deposit, a payor transfers money from his checking account to yours. This makes your money available more quickly and lowers the risk of the money being stolen.

No Premium Payments on Existing Insurance Policies. Most insurers cancel your policies when you fail to make the premium payment by the due date. Sometimes you can schedule automatic payments from your checking account. Make notes in your checkbook or diary to ensure that you make these important payments. Contact your insurance agent to find out whether he would contact you during the grace period before canceling your policy.

No Health Insurance Premiums. This protection is important to you and your family. If your employer does not offer health coverage, consider a health maintenance organization (HMO). If private health insurance is unavailable or impractical for you, currently 28 states sponsor health insurance programs.

No Health Care or Flexible Spending Account. Under this program, your employer deducts money from your paycheck to fund medical expenses which are not reimbursed by health insurance. Your payroll deductions are pre-tax and when you file a claim, your employer should reimburse you for qualifying expenses up to the lower of your expenses and total payroll deductions. You benefit by saving the income taxes on your reimbursements.

Eligible expenses include your deductible, co-payments, and non-reimbursable costs such as eyeglasses and dentistry. You must file claims for 1994 expenses by March 31, 1995 and if you don't use all the money in your flexible spending account by the deadline, you lose the remaining money in the account. The 1994 contribution limit is $3,000.

No Dependent Spending Account. Your employer may offer this account which enables you to save money on qualified care for your dependents such as day care services. This account works in the same fashion as the Flexible Spending Account explained above. The 1994 contribution limit is $5,000.

No Disability Insurance Premiums. Disability insurance replaces part of your income (generally ⅔) in the event you are injured and cannot work. The best policies contain these two features: **noncancelable**, which means that as long as you pay your premiums, the coverage is effective; and **portability**, which means that if you leave your company, if you continue paying the premiums, the coverage continues to be in effect. If your employer does not offer this coverage, contact your trade associations to see if they offer group policies.

No Catastrophic or Major Medical Insurance Premiums. These policies are relatively inexpensive and begin paying health insurance benefits when you hit the cap on your basic health insurance policy.

No Payments for Medical or Physical Examinations. It may be time to schedule a routine check-up. If you are under 35, you should have a complete physical at least once every three years, and once a year after you reach 35.

No Payments for Dentistry. Having your teeth cleaned by a dentist or hygienist helps prevent tooth decay. If you have dental insurance, most plans include two cleanings/check-ups per year. Even if you don't have dental insurance, paying for two cleanings per year may preserve your teeth and help you avoid costly and painful treatment later on.

No Quarterly Estimated Income Tax Payments. In most cases, in one year, taxpayers must pay taxes equal to the lesser of 100% of last year's Federal income tax bill and 90% of this year's liability; taxpayers who don't pay enough tax may face penalties. Individuals whose adjusted gross income exceeds $75,000 and whose income jumps by more than $40,000 must pay taxes equal to 90% of the current year's tax liability. If you are married, file a joint tax return and your adjusted gross income exceeds $150,000, you should avoid penalties by paying taxes of 110% of your last year's tax bill.

Your accountant can help calculate your tax bill. Be especially careful when your income or financial circumstances change significantly. As appropriate, adjust your withholdings and estimated income tax payments. Consider tax-advantaged investments such as owning a home, funding retirement plans, and investing in Treasury and municipal securities.

No Payments to Accountants for Income Tax Advice. A quality accountant can reduce your tax bill and help you comply with the ever-changing and complex tax laws. Accountants often charge

$200—$400 to prepare your income tax return and provide income tax advice. Seek referrals from your friends and family. An accountant's fee for tax preparation is generally deductible as a miscellaneous deduction on Schedule A of Form 1040.

Some accountants sell insurance and tax shelters, and when you buy financial products, the accountant earns commissions. This can represent a conflict of interest if the accountant recommends products that are not suitable for you. Consider an accountant for tax advice and a financial planner for investment advice.

No Mortgage Payments. Owning a home is often a family's most significant investment and in most cases, the related mortgage interest is still tax deductible under the Tax Reconciliation Act of 1993. If you don't own a home and are ready to settle down in a specific neighborhood, consider buying a home.

No Extra Mortgage Payments. Most home mortgages permit you to make extra mortgage payments without penalty. Payments in excess of the required monthly payment reduce the principal balance and the interest expense. Paying $25 extra every month on a $100,000, 30-year mortgage at a 10% interest rate, can save you $36,664 before taxes, and $25,665 after taxes at a 30% combined tax rate. When you pay $50 extra every month, you double your savings.

Generally, a mortgage is a relatively inexpensive borrowing, especially with the income tax deduction; so before making extra payments to your mortgage, pay down high cost credit card and other consumer debt.

In addition to paying down your mortgage, you can divide your monthly contractual payment in half and make two payments every month. Or, make half your monthly payment, every other week. Or consider using year-end bonuses and overtime pay to reduce your principal balance.

No Life Insurance Premiums. The best way to protect your family and your assets is to purchase term life insurance. When your family relies on your income, purchase term life insurance which pays benefits upon your death. Buy life insurance only to protect your heirs; generally, life insurance on children is not a worthwhile purchase.

Universal or Whole Life policies pay benefits upon your death and offer an investment program. Often, buying term insurance and investing through a tax-deferred retirement plan (401(k), 403(b), or IRA) can be more cost effective than buying whole life or universal life insurance policies.

No Homeowner's or Renter's Insurance Premiums. The best way to protect your home and your belongings is to purchase property and casualty insurance. You may be surprised to learn of the value of the contents of your home — a catastrophe could be disastrous. Buy **replacement cost insurance** which replaces your belongings at their current cost, up to the maximum face value of the policy.

Every year, review your coverage in relation to the current replacement cost of your belongings and raise your coverage as appropriate. Every year, photograph or videotape the contents of your home to prove the existence, nature and value of your belongings. Save the photos and store your receipts at a separate location such as a friend's house or safe deposit box.

No Premiums For Expensive Jewelry, Personal Computers, or Furs. Many homeowners or renters insurance policies cover jewelry and personal computers up to $1,000—$2,000. The coverage for furs varies by insurance policy. When the value of these special items exceeds your insurance policy limits, purchase riders which provide adequate coverage.

No Emergency Fund. It is important to accumulate a safety fund equal to 3—6 months of living expenses. The money might fund medical costs, automobile or appliance repairs, or

74

unemployment. Keep your emergency fund in a low-risk, high-quality money market account or money market mutual fund.

No Monthly Investments for Children's Education. The best way to help your children go to college is to invest money every month. When you have at least five years before your children enroll, choose a no-load diversified common stock mutual fund. Start as early as possible to benefit from compound returns.

Give money to your qualified dependents under the Uniform Gift to Minors Act (UGMA) and part or all of the income will be taxed at your child's (lower) tax rate. UGMA gifts are irrevocable. Consult your accountant first.

No Payments To Maintain Licenses and Certifications. Many professionals including accountants and teachers pay fees to maintain their licenses. Professional fees may be tax deductible as business expenses, so consult your accountant. Other such important documents with expiration dates include passports and driver's licenses. Make reminder notes in your checkbook or diary to meet these important deadlines.

No Payments for Servicing Your Car. To extend your car's life, your mechanic should perform a routine check-up, servicing, and oil change every three months or 3,000 miles, whichever occurs earlier. Rotate your tires and perform tune-ups as necessary.

SUMMARY:
So, now you don't see it.

This chapter described transactions which are symptomatic of financial health. These transactions should appear in your checkbook to help you improve your financial position. Every year, scan your checkbook for these items, and if they don't appear, set them up. Then, you will save more money and build more wealth.

It's the holiday season, and the last thing you want to do is review your checkbook.   Okay — wait until January, but performing an annual review in September or October may save you money now and help you plan ahead for the upcoming year.

Scan All of This Year's Transactions to Save More Money Next Year.   Review your entire checkbook, even when you use a consistent coding system.   Look for transactions where you wasted money.   Can you avoid the inefficient and wasteful transactions and repeat the successful transactions next year?

What are the three largest expense categories?   Can you eliminate transactions or reduce your expenses to save money? Will some of the major transactions and expenses appear next year also?   Can you plan ahead and save money to meet these expenses and avoid credit card debt and cash crunches?

Have your financial circumstances changed from last year?   Is it time to restructure your investments or expenses?

Take Advantage of Changes in Tax Law or Changing Income Status.   Defer or accelerate income and tax deductions depending on your circumstances and the laws in effect.   By paying tax-deductible expenses this year, you can realize the deduction in the current year and reduce your tax bill.   Similarly, you could defer the payment until next year which would reduce this year's deductions, increase this year's income and reduce next year's income.   Consult your accountant.

Plan Ahead for Upcoming Major Expenditures.   Most major expenses are predictable and you may be able to plan ahead and set money aside.   Some of these major outlays include weddings, having a baby, medical treatment, buying a house or car, back-to-school expenses, tuition, home repairs, home appliances, and costs related to starting a business. These costs often exceed ongoing monthly spending. **Anticipate these expenses as early as possible and reduce your out-of-pocket and credit card spending at least 2—6 months before the date of the expenditure to save enough money to cover the outlays and avoid incurring consumer debt**.

When you save money and plan to use it in the near future, use a low risk, money market account or mutual fund to preserve your principal, not earn the highest rate of return.

Are There Any Medical Expenses Which Are Covered By Your Insurance Which Have Not Been Reimbursed? Submit claims now to increase the likelihood of reimbursement, especially since many plans have reimbursement deadlines (often March 31 of the following year). Review chapter 6: Better Money Management and the example of Dr. Jeff.

Were Your Year-End Account Balances Higher or Lower Than the Balances at the Beginning of the Year? When your year-end account balances are lower than the balances at the beginning of the year, you may have spent more money than you earned or depleted your savings. Reduce your spending next year. Of course, if your year-end balances declined because you made investments or funded a retirement account, then your total wealth should be higher, and that's good.

Was Your Average Monthly Account Balance High Enough to Qualify for "Free Checking" or a NOW Account? If so, review chapter 8: Free or Not Free? and determine whether you should switch to these accounts or make other investments which better meet your objectives.

Can You Combine Different Account Balances to Meet the Financial Institution's Minimum Account Balance for Reduced Fee or "Free Checking"? If so, consider switching your account classification or making other alternative investments which offer higher rates of return.

Is your year-end checking account balance more than $1,000? If so and you don't need the money to cover your checks, transfer the extra money to a money market account or money market mutual fund to earn interest income.

How Much Overdraft Interest Expense Did You Pay This Year? If you paid more than $15 in overdraft interest expense this year, that's too much. Control your expenses and reduce your spending next year.

How Much Credit Card Debt Do You Have at Year-End? Usually, credit card debt is the result of excess consumer spending. But credit card debt is very costly. Unfortunately, credit card bills tend to increase rather than decrease, and the bills can stretch beyond our means easily. Review chapter 10: Now You See It for strategies for managing credit card debt.

When Did You Make Your IRA Contribution? Whenever possible, make your annual IRA contribution at the beginning of the new year. This strategy enables you to take greater advantage of compound returns.

Bad Investments. Unfortunately, many of us make investments which go sour. The key is to learn why our thinking was flawed and avoid the mistake in the future. Did you assume additional risk to achieve a higher rate of return?

Taking on higher risk may be okay as long as you are prepared to absorb the losses and continue to maintain a balanced and diversified portfolio. Perhaps you followed an investment advisor's high pressure sale or failed to conduct enough independent thorough research. Maybe you thought you received a "Hot Tip" which turned out to be old or false news.

Which Transactions Were Successful This Year? Scan your checkbook for transactions that helped you save money, build wealth or attain your financial goals. Definitely repeat those transactions next year.

Do you have an automatic monthly investment program? An automatic monthly investment program is the key to building wealth. If you don't fund a mutual fund every month, start such a program in early January. Review chapter 11: Now You Don't.

Which Transactions Were Fun? In the Spring of 1991, I studied improvisational comedy at Chicago City Limits in New York City (212-772-8707). My year-end checkbook analysis reminded me how much fun the class was and that I would like to enroll in another improv class soon. Make it a priority to repeat fun and rewarding activities.

Set New Year's Resolutions. Set one or two important financial goals for the upcoming year and create an action plan to attain those goals. You might decide to save $1,200 this year by reducing your spending and saving $100 every month or $25 every week. Other goals might include starting an investment program, reducing credit card debt, saving for retirement, or buying a new home.

SUMMARY:
Every year, make a year-end review of your checkbook. Your analytical review should help you see how you spend your money. Then, you can take steps to change your personal financial picture to save more money and build more wealth.

13. *SAFETY FIRST*

This chapter explains how to safeguard yourself, your money, ATM cards, checks, and checking accounts.

$ <u>Guard your ATM and credit cards carefully.</u> Your ATM and credit cards control access to your money. Record your card numbers and your financial institutions' phone numbers on a piece of paper and store your list in a safe and accessible place in your home — if you lose your ATM or credit card, you can cancel them quickly.

$ <u>Memorize your personal access code</u>. Never carry your ATM code in your wallet or pocketbook. If you lose your ATM card or it is stolen, a thief may gain access to your money. Never share your password with anyone. Most important, don't write your ATM code on your ATM card.

$ <u>Choose an access number that's not obvious or written on your other identification cards</u>. For example, many people choose code numbers that are easy to remember such as their home address or phone number; but these numbers often appear on identification cards they carry in their wallets. If you lose your wallet or someone picks your pocket, a thief may gain easy access to your money.

$ <u>When you use an ATM, don't let onlookers see your code number</u>. Thieves may watch you use the ATM machine, memorize your secret code and then steal your wallet and your money. And, don't leave an open purse dangling behind you where it can be pick-pocketed or stolen.

$ <u>Make cash withdrawals during daylight only</u>. For late-night cash withdrawals, visit ATMs located in supermarkets rather than financial institutions. At night there may be more activity at the supermarket than at stand-alone ATM machines at financial institutions. Start keeping $20—$100 of "safety money" in a secure place in your home.

$ Park your car in well-lit areas near the ATM machines. Parking near the ATM machine shortens the distance between your car and the ATM. This means you can spend less time in the parking lot and are more likely to avoid trouble.

$ Don't use the ATM machines when you sense trouble. When you see strangers loitering around the ATM area, leave immediately. Often, thieves stand near ATM machines or in parking lots waiting for an opportunity to steal your money. When you sense trouble, walk away quietly and quickly. Return later or visit another ATM.

$ Don't show any strangers how to use your ATM card. **Popular scam**: a seemingly innocent bystander or foreigner pretends to be lost or confused and asks you to show him how to use his ATM card. The thief asks you to demonstrate how to use **your** ATM card and then memorizes your personal code. He asks to try your card and subtly switches your card for a phoney one. Later on, he steals your money.

$ Avoid ATM machines in dark, unusual, or out of the way places. Instead, use ATMs located in busy areas. Use only official ATM machines in financial institutions, supermarkets, and other reputable places. There have been cases where thieves installed phoney ATM machines in shopping malls. The machines recorded people's ATM card numbers. Then the thieves manufactured fake ATM cards and made fraudulent cash withdrawals.

$ Don't let strangers into the ATM area. This may seem rude, especially in your neighborhood, but there are many troublemakers around today — keep yourself and your money as safe as possible.

$ Don't leave any trash behind at the ATM machine. Recently, thieves have created fake ATM cards from ATM receipts by decoding the ATM card number. Take all your receipts and papers with you. Tear them up and discard them at home.

$ <u>Use the ATMs quickly and leave</u>. Make a list of transactions you want to make and prepare your deposit slips at home. Remove your ATM card from your wallet when you are still in the car so you will not have to fumble to find it. Count your money in private, quickly, while you stand at the ATM; then stuff the money and your ATM card into your pocket, wallet, or purse. Always close your pocketbook before you leave the ATM area and hold the strap tightly. These steps should help you spend less time at the ATM machine and reduce your vulnerability to crime.

$ <u>If you lose an ATM or credit card,</u> <u>call your financial institution immediately and cancel it</u>. Your liability for money fraudulently withdrawn (stolen) from your account varies depending on when you report the theft or loss of your ATM card. Under the Federal Electronic Funds Transfer Act, when you lose your ATM card and notify your financial institution within two days of the loss, your liability should be limited to $50. When you notify your financial institution after two days, your liability may jump to $500.

When unauthorized transfers appear on your statement, notify your financial institution immediately. Unapproved transfers can arise from computer errors or fraud.

Contact your financial institutions now to learn their policies regarding your liability and lost ATM cards.

$ <u>Keep a current list or photocopy of the contents of your wallet at home</u>. A photocopy of the contents of your wallet provides a complete record of your financial and identification cards. Write the phone numbers of your credit card companies and financial institutions next to the card numbers so you can cancel the cards quickly if you lose your wallet or purse.

$ <u>Subscribe to a credit card loss prevention service</u>. These services manage databases that store all your credit card numbers in a central computer file. If you lose your wallet, with one call you can cancel all your cards and order replacements. Contact your financial institution's credit card customer service center to see if they offer this service. If you subscribe to this service, update your records whenever your card numbers change.

Service	Telephone Number
Protection Plus® (Citibank®)	1-800-833-7740
Credit Card Sentinel	1-800-423-5166

$ Sign up for direct deposit service. Your employer, pension plan administrator or the Social Security Administration deposits your paycheck directly into your checking account and the funds should become available as "cash" more quickly. This also saves you the trouble of running to the financial institution to deposit your check.

$ Write your checks legibly. When the amount of a check, as presented in numbers, differs from the amount written in words, the financial institution completes the transaction for the amount in words. To prevent a thief from altering your checks, always use horizontal lines to fill blank space:

"$Two hundred and xx/100 ≡ ≡ ≡ ≡ ≡ ≡ ≡ ≡ ≡ ≡ ≡ ≡ ≡"

$ Use restrictive endorsements, especially if you deposit checks in an ATM machine. A restrictive endorsement limits how a check can be used. The words "for deposit only" along with your account number and signature mean the check can be deposited in your account only.

$ Don't carry blank checks in your wallet or carry them only when you plan to use them. Although I recommended keeping blank checks in your wallet, carrying checks in your wallet increases the risk of losing checks, having to place stop payment orders, and a thief drawing checks on your account. If you lose your wallet, place stop orders on all your unaccounted for checks and close your checking account.

$ <u>Report check forgeries within 14 days after your financial institution mails your account statement</u>. Generally, if you notify your financial institution within 14 days, you will receive 100% reimbursement for the loss; if not, you may bear subsequent losses. If you notify your financial institution within 14 days, you may not have to place stop payment orders on all your missing checks.

$ <u>Store important papers in a safe deposit or vault box</u>. Such papers include: birth, marriage and death certificates; divorce or separation agreements; securities (stocks, bonds), contracts and other legal papers; mortgage documents; titles to real estate, homes, boats and automobiles; photos or videotapes of your home and possessions for insurance purposes.

Don't store wills, valuables or cash in a vault box. Some people use safe deposit boxes to store cash. Upon the box-holder's death, the financial institution seals the box until the tax authorities determine the contents. Regarding cash you store in your vault box, the IRS presumes you have not paid income taxes on the money, and this could lead to legal troubles.

Beware: the financial institution's insurance coverage on the contents of a vault box is low, so review your homeowner's policy. To collect any insurance proceeds in an event of loss, you must be able to prove what you lost. Always keep accurate records of the contents of your safe deposit box and get witnesses to attest to the contents of the box.

<u>SUMMARY</u>: There are many thieves and scam artists looking to steal your money. Take precautions and be careful; handle yourself, your money and your accounts carefully and safely.

14. *CHAOTIC RECORDS*

Sometimes a checkbook can become a total mess. Perhaps several months have elapsed since you made your last entry or maybe your records are in a state of disarray. You can take these few simple steps to get your checkbook back on track.

1 Obtain your checking account statements for the months you decide to reconcile.

2 Record all your checks, deposits, fees and charges and cash withdrawals in your checkbook in chronological order.

3 Then, calculate your account balance.

If you discarded your ATM receipts from cash withdrawals, copy the total cash withdrawals from your checking account statements into your checkbook. You can verify your cash withdrawals by making sure you actually executed your transactions at the ATM machines at the addresses listed on your account statements.

You can verify your payroll deposits by comparing your account statements with your paycheck stubs.

4 If your checking account does not reconcile to the monthly statement, add or subtract the difference between your calculated checkbook balance and your financial institution's calculation of your account balance. Make an entry in your checkbook called "account balance adjustment" to reconcile your calculated checkbook balance to your financial institution's account balance. You may need to perform this step for several months until all your transactions clear your checking account and you can reconcile your checkbook as described in chapter 7: Balancing The Books.

5 If step 4 fails, stop using your checkbook for 2—3 months and record all new transactions on separate sheets of paper or in a new checkbook. When you reconcile the monthly activity, copy the items that appear on your monthly account statement from the sheets of paper into your checkbook; then reconcile your account as described in chapter 7: Balancing The Books. Within a few months, all your transactions should clear your account and you should be able to reconcile your checking account.

6 If all else fails, don't worry about it. Enter all your new transactions, fees and charges in your checkbook and calculate your account balance. Going forward, enter all of your transactions in your checkbook. Eventually, all your transactions should clear your account and your account balance should become closer to your account statement. Then, repeat step #4 above.

$ <u>Send your complaints directly to the president of the financial institution</u>. Several years ago, I was having trouble obtaining the proper checking account classification and fee treatment. Once I wrote to the president of the company, the difficulty was corrected immediately.

$ <u>Deposit cash with a teller</u>. Tellers will count your money, verify your deposits, and issue receipts. You should be able to correct any discrepancies immediately.

$ <u>Pay important business and tax deductible expenses by check</u>. Checks provide better documentation to substantiate your income tax deductions. Save the original receipts and write detailed descriptions of the transactions.

$ <u>Set up a separate checking account for your business</u>. Although two checking accounts increase your fees, two sets of records help you separate personal and business expenses. When you borrow money and use the proceeds for business purposes, a separate business checking account should help substantiate the tax deductibility of the interest expense.

$ <u>Photocopy important checks before mailing them</u>. This provides complete records for tax and insurance purposes. This is very important for payments to the IRS, investments, major purchases such as a car, house, appliances, and home improvements. I find it helpful to photocopy checks I receive from income tax refunds and business activities.

$ <u>When you buy a personal residence, write a separate check for the mortgage points to preserve the income tax deduction</u>. The Tax Act of 1986 allows borrowers to itemize the points on their home mortgage but requires the borrower to pay the points with a separate check; as opposed to borrowing the money for the points as part of the mortgage.

$ Don't make checks payable to "cash". Financial institutions cash checks payable to "cash" without an endorsement from the recipient of the money. You won't have a record of the purpose of the payment or proof that the payee received the money.

$ Beware of the words "Accord & Satisfaction" or "Partial Payment as Payment in Full". Sometimes, debtors send checks for partial payment of an obligation and write on the check "accord and satisfaction". According to the law, this means that once the check is cashed or deposited, the recipient agrees to accept the amount of the check as full payment for the debt. **DON'T deposit these checks** and consult your lawyer. Notify the debtor and seek the remainder of the money due.

$ Draw a will. A will helps you organize your financial affairs and provide for a more orderly distribution of your assets after your death. Most important, you can better provide for your family.

$ Use your checkbook as a memory device to flag important and major transactions. Write reminder notes in your checkbook, several pages ahead of the current page, to meet important deadlines and ensure that you make major payments. This should enable you to prepare for the expenditure.

$ Hesitate before implementing computer checking. Some people use computer programs to manage their checking accounts. While computers can be useful to print checks and track expenses, often, computers complicate simple activities and consume more time than they provide valuable information. There are two general types of computer checking and one electronic check-printing calculator:

1 Personal computer money management software programs. These programs can be helpful for printing checks and tracking expenses but most people's personal financial situations do not warrant using a computer. Besides, entering the data can be time consuming. The software programs reconcile your checking account but can be inflexible regarding errors because they are designed to accept certain entries. The two most popular programs are: Quicken® by Intuit™, and Kiplinger's CA—Simply Money. Visit a local software store or call Egghead Software (1-800-344-4323).

2 Pay expenses by computer through your financial institution or with Prodigy®. With a computer modem, you can access your accounts, pay bills, and transfer and invest money; you can even schedule monthly bills for payment. Most major vendors participate in the Federal wire transfer payment system, and for those who don't, your financial institution can write checks to pay those bills. This type of computer checking eliminates the need for checks but can be costly. Despite the fees, some people I know welcome the opportunity not to write checks.

3 Panasonic's C.P.A. Check Printing Accountant™ can help you manage your checking account. You can insert 25 personal checks into the calculator and the machine will print your checks. The calculator will track your account balance and print transaction summaries but cannot reconcile your account. For more information or to order, call Hammacher Schlemmer (1-800-421-9002).

Computerized checking is a personal preference. I'm okay with my handwritten check register, my calculator, and the Two Color System.

16. ONE FINAL STRATEGY FOR SAVING MONEY

The first step to saving more money and building more wealth is to set a financial goal. The specific goals are not important as long as the goals are important to you. Checkbook Management illustrated how to unlock your checkbook's value to help you attain your financial goals.

- Enter all your financial transactions in your checkbook and calculate a running balance.

- Review your checkbook and make a list of important action steps you plan to take to achieve your financial goals.

- Keep your checkbook up-to-date; then your checkbook should provide valuable financial information to help you manage your money and attain your financial goals.

- Implement your plan and stick with it so you will attain your financial goals.

Even though you are about to close this guide, don't forget all the ideas you thought of as you read Checkbook Management and its usefulness for your personal finances. From time to time, pull this guide off the shelf and review the strategies and tactics compared with your current personal financial practices, checkbook and current financial position. Then take action to save more money and build more wealth.

I look forward to hearing your thoughts and experiences. Best wishes for financial success,

Eric Gelb
c/o Career Advancement Center, Inc.™
Post Office Box 436
Woodmere, New York 11598-0436

TELEPHONE DIRECTORY

Travellers Checks & Money Wire Services
American Express® Travellers Checks 1-800-673-3782
American Express® Moneygrams 1-800-543-4080
Citicorp® Travellers Checks 1-800-645-6556
Thomas Cook Travellers Checks 1-800-223-7373
Western Union (money wire service) 1-800-325-6000

Long Distance Telephone Services
ATT 1-800-225-5288
MCI® 1-800-444-4444
Metromedia® 1-800-275-0200
Sprint® 1-800-877-4646

Magazines and Publications
Business Week Magazine 1-800-635-1200
Forbes Magazine 1-800-888-9896
Money® Magazine 1-800-336-0079
Morningstar Mutual Funds (analysis) 1-800-876-5005
Smart Money Magazine 1-800-444-4204

Mutual Fund Families
Janus Mutual Funds 1-800-525-8983
Twentieth Century Investors 1-800-345-2021
USAA 1-800-292-8706

Purchasing Checks Through The Mail
Checks in the Mail™ 1-800-733-4443
Current Check Printers 1-800-533-3973
Custom Direct Check Printers 1-800-272-5432

Other
Chicago City Limits (New York City) 1-212-772-8707
Credit Card Sentinel 1-800-423-5166
Credit Union National Association 1-800-358-5710
Egghead Computer Software (mail order) 1-800-344-4323
Federal Deposit Insurance Corp (FDIC) 1-800-424-5488
Internal Revenue Service 1-800-829-3676
Protection Plus® (Citibank's credit card service) . . 1-800-833-7740
Veribanc (financial research firm) 1-617-245-8370

INDEX

THE CAREER ADVANCEMENT CENTER CATALOG

Personal Budget Planner — A Guide for Financial Success
by Eric Gelb
Straightforward financial advice. Blends anecdotes with solid
examples. Financial tables encourage know-how rather than
vague speculations and theories. "Exhaustive in its efforts to
help readers gain control of their finances." says Inc. magazine.

106 pages; $19.95

The Instant Millionaire by Mark Fisher
Wonderful fable about self-empowerment and how to become a
millionaire. The story of a young man who discovers how to
take control of his destiny and acquire true wealth.

132 pages; $8.95

Change Your Job, Change Your Life! — High Impact Strategies
For Finding Great Jobs in the 90s by Dr. Ronald L. Krannich
Filled with advice on how to spot jobs of tomorrow, how to best
determine your capabilities, and how to communicate your
qualifications. "A truly impressive book." — Career
Opportunities News   363 pages; $14.95

Dynamite Answers to Interview Questions by Drs. Caryl & Ron
Krannich — Includes sample answers to hundreds of questions
interviewers ask in the critical job interview. Shows how to turn
possible negative responses into positive answers that can mean
the difference between being accepted or rejected for the job.

166 pages; $9.95

Teach Your Child the Value of Money by Harold & Sandy Moe
Excellent guide for parents who want to help their children get
an early start on managing their money. Hundreds of ideas,
hints, How-Tos, and action tips guide you in helping your
children master their financial future.

128 pages; $7.95

CAREER ADVANCEMENT CENTER ORDER FORM

☎ Telephone Orders: Call our order center toll-free: 1-800-669-0773. Please have your Mastercard or Visa card ready.

🕑 FAX Orders: 515-472-3186.

✉ By Mail: Career Advancement Center, Box 436, Woodmere, NY 11598-0436. Make checks payable to Career Advancement Center, Inc.

Please send the following books. I understand that I may return any books for a full refund for any reason — no questions asked.

Title	Qty	Price	Total
Personal Budget Planner by Eric Gelb		$19.95	
Checkbook Management by Eric Gelb		$6.50	
The Instant Millionaire by Mark Fisher		$8.95	
Change Your Job, Change Your Life! by Dr. Ronald L. Krannich		$14.95	
Dynamite Answers to Interview Questions by Drs. Caryl & Ron Krannich		$9.95	
Teach Your Child the Value of Money by Harold & Sandy Moe		$7.95	
Total Order Price:			
Shipping & Handling:			$3.00
Sales Tax (NYS & NYC residents):			
Total:			

Name:	
Address:	
City/State/Zip Code:	

Credit Card signature:	
Card # & Expiration Date:	

Please allow 4—6 weeks for delivery.